# REJECTION SENSITIVE DYSPHORIA WORKBOOK

Therapeutic Worksheets for Overcoming Emotional Fragility and Rejection Sensitivity in Relationships

**DARIO GARDELLA**

COPYRIGHT © 2025

### NOTICE THE PAINFUL THOUGHT
WHEN YOU FEEL HURT, PAUSE AND LISTEN TO THE THOUGHT RUNNING THROUGH YOUR MIND, LIKE: "I'M NOT GOOD ENOUGH."
ACKNOWLEDGE THE PAIN WITHOUT JUDGMENT.

### CHALLENGE THE THOUGHT
### GENTLY ASK YOURSELF:
"AM I IMAGINING THE WORST?"
"IS IT POSSIBLE THERE'S ANOTHER REASON FOR THIS SITUATION?"

### REFRAME THE THOUGHT
GENTLY SHIFT THE THOUGHT TO A KINDER PERSPECTIVE ?
TREAT YOURSELF WITH THE SAME COMPASSION YOU'D SHOW A FRIEND.

### CALM YOUR EMOTIONS
IF THE HURT FEELS OVERWHELMING, USE DEEP BREATHING AND GROUNDING TECHNIQUES TO EASE THE INTENSITY ?

### FIND HEALTHY DISTRACTIONS
TAKE CARE OF YOURSELF BY ENGAGING IN ACTIVITIES THAT HELP SHIFT YOUR FOCUS?

### REFLECT AND GROW
AS YOU MOVE FORWARD, LOOK BACK ON MOMENTS OF HURT.

- - - - - - - - - - - -

### REFLECT ON:
WAS THE PAIN AS BAD AS IT FELT IN THE MOMENT?
HOW DID YOU FEEL AFTER TAKING A STEP BACK?

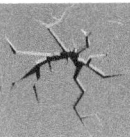

# CRITICAL SENSITIVITY WORKSHEET

## 1. WHAT HAPPENED?
- THINK OF A SITUATION WHERE YOU FELT HURT BY REJECTION OR CRITICISM.
- WRITE IT DOWN, AS IF YOU WERE TELLING A CLOSE FRIEND.
- DESCRIBE THE SURROUNDING EVENTS (WHO WAS MOST INVOLVED IN THE PROBLEM AND WHAT WAS SAID THAT HURT YOU? AND HOW DID YOU REACT EMOTIONALLY, ANGRY AND SAD!

## 2. TAKE A MOMENT
- NOW, LET'S LOOK AT IT FROM A DIFFERENT ANGLE. DO YOU THINK THE OTHER PERSON MEANT TO HURT YOU? _WAS THE HURT CENTERED AROUND THE CONFLICT BETWEEN YOU (PERSONAL, NOT GENERAL)?_
- IF THIS HAPPENED TO A CLOSE FRIEND, HOW WOULD YOU DEAL WITH THEM SO THAT THEY FEEL BETTER ABOUT THE EMOTIONAL DAMAGE CAUSED BY THIS INCIDENT?
- WRITE YOUR PERSPECTIVE ON THE INCIDENT FROM A LOGICAL, NOT EMOTIONAL, PERSPECTIVE?

## 3. WHAT CAN YOU DO NEXT TIME?
- WHEN YOU FACE REJECTION OR CRITICISM AGAIN, HOW CAN YOU DEAL WITH YOURSELF LOVINGLY SO THAT YOU DON'T GET EMOTIONALLY HURT? REMEMBER, IT'S NOT THE END OF THE WORLD. WE ALL GET EMOTIONALLY HURT.
- WHAT BELIEFS DO YOU NEED TO ARM YOURSELF WITH TO STAY GROUNDED? WRITE DOWN ONE OR TWO IDEAS YOU'D LIKE TO TRY NEXT TIME

## 4. A LITTLE KINDNESS TO YOURSELF
- WHAT ARE SOME KIND, ADAPTIVE PHRASES YOU CAN SAY TO YOURSELF? AFTER ANY FUTURE POSITION?

# CRITICAL SENSITIVITY
## WORKSHEET

# MINDFULNESS WORKSHEET FOR LOW SELF-ESTEEM RSD-ADHD

INTRUSIVE THOUGHTS ABOUT REJECTION CAN FEEL PAINFUL WHENEVER THEY COME TO MIND. BUT REST ASSURED, OBSERVING THEM WITHOUT JUDGING THEM WILL LESSEN THEIR EMOTIONAL INTENSITY. THEY ARE SIMPLY A REFLECTION OF OTHER PEOPLE'S BEHAVIORS TOWARD A SITUATION YOU'VE BEEN INVOLVED IN.

IMAGINE THESE INTRUSIVE THOUGHTS AS A LEAF FLOATING IN A STREAM (A RIVER, FOR EXAMPLE). OBSERVE THEM WITHOUT PUSHING THEM AWAY.

REPEAT THIS EXERCISE FOR A FEW MOMENTS, LETTING EACH THOUGHT SLIP THROUGH YOUR MIND LIKE A LEAF GENTLY MOVING THROUGH THE WATER UNTIL IT REACHES THE END OF THE RIVER AND DISAPPEARS COMPLETELY.

HAVE YOU NOTICED ANY CHANGES IN YOUR FEELINGS BY APPLYING THIS EXERCISE FOR DISTURBING AND PAINFUL THOUGHTS?

- **WRITE ABOUT THIS EXPERIENCE AND MAKE A PLAN FOR MANAGING INTRUSIVE THOUGHTS RESULTING FROM PREVIOUS EXPERIENCES OF HARSH CRITICISM!**

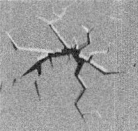

# UNDERSTANDING AND OVERCOMING SOCIAL CHALLENGES

## EXPLINATIONS :

THIS WORKSHEET WILL HELP YOU EXPLORE SOCIAL CHALLENGES LIKE FEELING LEFT OUT OR MISUNDERSTOOD AND ADDRESSES THE NEED FOR APPROVAL AND REASSURANCE.

### 1. IDENTIFYING SOCIAL CHALLENGES:

- THINK ABOUT TIMES WHEN YOU FELT LEFT OUT OR LIKE OTHERS DIDN'T UNDERSTAND YOU.
- HOW DID THAT MAKE YOU FEEL? WHAT WAS YOUR REACTION IN THOSE MOMENTS?

### 2. RECOGNIZING THE NEED FOR APPROVAL

- REFLECT ON WHAT HELPS YOU FEEL CONFIDENT AND SECURE.
- HOW DO YOU USUALLY COPE WHEN YOU DON'T RECEIVE THE REASSURANCE YOU'RE LOOKING FOR FROM OTHERS?

### 3. ANALYZING PATTERNS:

- HAVE YOU NOTICED ANY PATTERNS IN YOUR RELATIONSHIPS WHEN YOU'VE FELT EXCLUDED?
- HOW DOES WANTING APPROVAL SHAPE THE WAY YOU CONNECT WITH OR RESPOND TO PEOPLE?

### 4. REFRAMING THOUGHTS:

- THINK OF A TIME YOU HAD A NEGATIVE THOUGHT ABOUT FEELING LEFT OUT. HOW COULD YOU REFRAME THAT THOUGHT INTO SOMETHING MORE POSITIVE OR HELPFUL?

# EXPRESSING YOURSELF AND ROLE-PLAYING 01

## OBJECTIVE:

THIS WORKSHEET HELPS YOU REFLECT ON HOW YOU RESPOND IN VULNERABLE SITUATIONS LIKE REJECTION OR CRITICISM AND PRACTICE MANAGING EMOTIONAL REACTIONS EFFECTIVELY. BY ROLE-PLAYING SCENARIOS, YOU CAN IMPROVE COMMUNICATION SKILLS AND EMOTIONAL RESILIENCE.

## SCENARIO 1: RECEIVING HARSH FEEDBACK FROM YOUR BOSS

## SITUATION:

YOU RECEIVE HARSH FEEDBACK ON A REPORT FROM YOUR BOSS. IT FEELS PERSONAL, BUT IT'S AN OPPORTUNITY FOR GROWTH.

## RESPONSE STRATEGY:

1. **RESPONSE STRATEGY:**
2. **DON'T PERSONALIZE THE MATTER. PAUSE AND BREATHE:** I WILL TAKE A MOMENT TO REST AND BREATHE DEEPLY FOR A LONG TIME WITHOUT TENSION AND WITHOUT THINKING ABOUT THE MOMENT IN ORDER TO GET RID OF NEGATIVE THOUGHTS FROM MY MIND DUE TO THE INTENSITY OF THE SITUATION.
3. **RE-PHRASE THE MATTER:** I MUST VIEW THE COMMENTS AS IMPORTANT, AS PROFESSIONAL AND NOT PERSONAL.
4. **ASK FOR CLARIFICATION:** IN ORDER NOT TO ESCALATE THE SITUATION, I MUST POLITELY ASK THE MANAGER FOR SPECIFIC DETAILS TO UNDERSTAND AREAS FOR IMPROVEMENT WITHOUT PERSONALIZING THINGS.
5. **ACT CONSTRUCTIVELY:** IF I NOTICE THAT THE MANAGER IS SOMEWHAT CALM, I MUST BRING UP THE TOPIC OF POLITENESS IN TALKING TO ME IN THE FUTURE BECAUSE THIS WILL DEEPEN COMMUNICATION AND UNDERSTANDING BETWEEN US.

## THERAPEUTIC REFLECTION:

LET'S IMAGINE THAT A SITUATION LIKE THIS HAPPENED TO YOU.

HOW WOULD YOU FEEL AND HOW WOULD YOU COPE? DEVELOP A SCENARIO?

## SCENARIO 2: DISCUSSING FEELINGS WITH A FRIEND

**SITUATION:**
YOU FEEL ISOLATED WHEN YOUR FRIENDS SPEND TIME WITHOUT YOU AND YOU WANT TO EXPRESS FEELINGS OF REJECTION IN THIS SITUATION.

**RESPONSE STRATEGY:**
**EXPRESS VULNERABILITY:** I WILL CLEARLY EXPLAIN HOW I FEEL WITHOUT PLACING BLAME. EXAMPLE: "I FELT HURT WHEN I SAW YOU ALL TOGETHER WITHOUT ME."

**BE OPEN:** I WILL LISTEN TO THEIR POINT OF VIEW ON THE MATTER. PERHAPS THERE WERE CIRCUMSTANCES THAT PREVENTED THEM FROM TELLING ME.

**FIND SOLUTIONS:** DESPITE THIS, I WILL NOT ALLOW FEELINGS OF REJECTION TO MAKE ME TEND TOWARDS ISOLATION IN THE FUTURE. THERE WILL BE OTHER PROGRAMS WITH FRIENDS. I WILL SEEK TO BE A MAIN FOCUS IN THEM.

**REFLECTION:**
LET'S IMAGINE THAT A SITUATION LIKE THIS HAPPENED TO YOU. HOW WOULD YOU FEEL AND HOW WOULD YOU COPE? DEVELOP A SCENARIO?

## SCENARIO 3: DEALING WITH ROMANTIC REJECTION

**SITUATION:**
YOU EXPRESS ROMANTIC INTEREST TO YOUR PARTNER BUT ARE REJECTED, MAKING YOU FEEL VULNERABLE, EXCLUDED, AND DEEPLY REJECTED.

**RESPONSE STRATEGY:**
**ACKNOWLEDGE YOUR EMOTIONS:** I WILL ALLOW MYSELF TO FEEL DISAPPOINTED BUT AVOID TAKING IT PERSONALLY.
**EXPRESS GRATITUDE:** HOWEVER, I SHOULD THANK THE OTHER PARTY FOR THEIR HONESTY RATHER THAN HIDE SOME NEGATIVES THAT MAY LEAD TO FURTHER DAMAGE TO THE RELATIONSHIP IN THE FUTURE.
**THERAPEUTIC REFLECTION:**
AFTER SEEING THE CORRECT WAY TO DEAL WITH REJECTION, WHAT ARE THE SHORTCOMINGS RELATED TO EMOTIONAL AND PSYCHOLOGICAL INTELLIGENCE THAT YOU HAVE LEARNED ABOUT YOURSELF?

- **WHAT CAN YOU LEARN FROM THIS APPROACH TO DEAL WITH REJECTION IN A HEALTHY WAY IN THE FUTURE? AND WHAT PLAN DO YOU HAVE IN MIND TO ACHIEVE THIS?**

# RSD-ADHD
# OPPOSITE ACTION PLAN WORKSHEET

*THIS WORKSHEET IS INTENDED TO HELP YOU ACT AGAINST UNHELPFUL EMOTIONAL URGES, ESPECIALLY THOSE THAT MAY LEAD TO ISOLATION, AVOIDANCE, OR IMPULSIVE BEHAVIORS. DIRECTIONS: WHEN YOU FEEL A STRONG EMOTION (ESPECIALLY AN ADHD-RELATED EMOTION SUCH AS REJECTION), IDENTIFY AN OPPOSING ACTION—SOMETHING THAT HELPS BALANCE THE URGE. FOLLOW THE PLAN BELOW.*

| Emotions | Emotion Urge (What do you want to do?) | Opposite Action (What can you do instead?) | How Do You Feel After? |
|---|---|---|---|
| Rejection | Isolate, avoid people or situations | Reach out to a friend, attend a social activity. | |
| Anger Lash out or withdraw | Lash out or withdraw. | Take a deep breath, pause, and use "I feel" statements. | |
| Sadness | s Stay in bed, avoid tasks | Go for a walk, engage in a hobby, or call someone. | |
| Frustration Quit | give up. | Break tasks into smaller steps, continue with patience. | |
| Fear/Anxiety | Avoid the feared situation | Face the fear in small, manageable steps. | |
| Shame | Hide or feel unworthy | journal about positive aspects of self. | |

THIS WORKSHEET IS INTENDED TO HELP YOU ACT AGAINST UNHELPFUL EMOTIONAL URGES, ESPECIALLY THOSE THAT MAY LEAD TO ISOLATION, AVOIDANCE, OR IMPULSIVE BEHAVIORS. DIRECTIONS: WHEN YOU FEEL A STRONG EMOTION (ESPECIALLY AN ADHD-RELATED EMOTION SUCH AS REJECTION), IDENTIFY AN OPPOSING ACTION—SOMETHING THAT HELPS BALANCE THE URGE. FOLLOW THE PLAN BELOW !

# DAILY / WEEKLY

# THERAPEUTIC PLAN

## FOR OVERCOMING RSD TRAITS

THESE INTERACTIVE, GUIDED PRACTICES WILL BE YOUR GUIDE TO BUILDING BEHAVIORAL BALANCE, ELIMINATING EMOTIONAL FRAGILITY, UNDERSTANDING YOUR CONDITION WELL, AND MAKING URGENT CHANGES IN YOUR PERSONALITY AND HOW YOU RESPOND TO SITUATIONS THAT REQUIRE EMOTIONAL STABILITY, STEP BY STEP. THIS MEANS THAT YOU WILL PARTICIPATE IN ACTIVITIES EVERY DAY OR WEEK THAT ARE CONSISTENT WITH YOUR LIFESTYLE AND ROUTINE TO FACE SOCIAL SITUATIONS WHERE YOU FEEL ANXIOUS ABOUT REJECTION, WHICH GIVES YOU THE OPPORTUNITY TO STUDY AND ANALYZE THE COPING STRATEGIES THAT SUIT YOU TO OVERCOME REJECTION SENSITIVITY, AND FORMULATE EFFECTIVE THERAPEUTIC GOALS INSPIRED BY YOUR EXPERIENCES.

# RSD-ADHD
# OPPOSITE ACTION PLAN WORKSHEET

*THIS WORKSHEET IS INTENDED TO HELP YOU ACT AGAINST UNHELPFUL EMOTIONAL URGES, ESPECIALLY THOSE THAT MAY LEAD TO ISOLATION, AVOIDANCE, OR IMPULSIVE BEHAVIORS. DIRECTIONS: WHEN YOU FEEL A STRONG EMOTION (ESPECIALLY AN ADHD-RELATED EMOTION SUCH AS REJECTION), IDENTIFY AN OPPOSING ACTION—SOMETHING THAT HELPS BALANCE THE URGE. FOLLOW THE PLAN BELOW.*

| Emotions | Emotion Urge (What do you want to do?) | Opposite Action (What can you do instead?) | How Do You Feel After? |
|---|---|---|---|
|  |  |  |  |
|  |  |  |  |
|  |  |  |  |
|  |  |  |  |
|  |  |  |  |
|  |  |  |  |

# RSD
# INTERACTIONS WORKSHEET

START YOUR DAY WITH A POSITIVE AFFIRMATION AND TACKLE A SMALL, SIMPLE TASK TO GIVE YOURSELF A QUICK SENSE OF ACCOMPLISHMENT. BREAK LARGER TASKS INTO MANAGEABLE STEPS AND SET TIMERS FOR FOCUSED WORK, TAKING SHORT BREAKS IN BETWEEN TO AVOID FEELING OVERWHELMED. REGULARLY CHECK IN WITH YOUR EMOTIONS, ESPECIALLY AFTER TASKS, AND BE KIND TO YOURSELF IF FEELINGS OF REJECTION OR FRUSTRATION ARISE—IT'S OKAY TO FEEL THOSE THINGS. ACKNOWLEDGE ANY CHALLENGES, AND END THE DAY WITH A POSITIVE AFFIRMATION.

Sleep Quality:

## MOOD TRACKER ✔

- ANGRY ☐
- UPSET ☐
- ANXIOUS ☐
- EMBARRASSED ☐
- UNCOMFORTABLE ☐
- BRAVE ☐
- CALM ☐
- JOYFUL ☐
- PEACEFUL ☐
- CONFUSED ☐
- DISCOURAGED ☐
- DISTRACTED ☐
- EMBARRASSED ☐
- EXCITED ☐
- FRIENDLY ☐
- GUILTY ☐
- HAPPY ☐
- HOPEFUL ☐
- LONELY ☐
- LOVED ☐
- NERVOUS ☐
- OFFENDED ☐
- SCARED ☐
- THOUGHTFUL ☐
- TIRED ☐
- UNCOMFORTABLE ☐
- INSECURE ☐

⊘ ___ : ___

⊘ ___ : ___

## THINGS TO WORK ON

# OVERCOMING RSD
# PRACTICAL WORKSHEET

Engage in a social situation that you think will enhance your RSD symptoms. Try to interact in a healthy way and remain in control of your feelings outwardly without withdrawing or getting angry. Maintain your self-respect and faith in yourself in situations that require this.
Be bold and engage in situations that reinforce your preconceived sense of failure. Gradually exposing and analyzing these situations enables you to get rid of psychological fragility, build your self-esteem, and gain social intelligence.

| WRITE THE MOST IMPORTANT DETAILS OF THE SITUATION IN THE CORRESPONDING BOX. | EVALUATE YOUR REACTIONS AND INTERACTIONS. (GOOD DEALING AND BAD DEALING) |
|---|---|
|  |  |

# EXPOSURE THERAPY
# FOR RSD TRAITS

Before engaging in social situations that might trigger RSD, take a moment to plan how you will handle potential emotional triggers. You may want to remind yourself that every comment or interaction is not a reflection of your worth, and that it's okay to step back if you start to feel overwhelmed. Visualizing how you would react to certain situations can help reduce anxiety and give you a sense of control. After the event, use the second part of the chart to assess how well you managed your emotional responses to perceived rejection or criticism, and to assess your level of control over any triggers.

## WHAT SHOULD I DO :

| | |
|---|---|
| | Evaluating my success rate in controlling feelings of rejection or criticism<br><br>○ ○ ○ ○ ○ |
| | Evaluating my success rate in showing balance and self-respect<br><br>○ ○ ○ ○ ○ |
| | Evaluating my success rate in avoiding false perfection to avoid failure<br><br>○ ○ ○ ○ ○ |

## NOTES

# RSD DIALECTICAL WORKSHEET

*Date* ............................................

CHALLENGE AND CORRECT NEGATIVE BEHAVIOR PATTERNS
AND THOUGHTS

ON THIS WORKSHEET, START THINKING ABOUT YOUR TRIGGERS FOR ANXIETY, EXCESSIVE SHYNESS, REJECTION SENSITIVITY, AND CONFLICTING VALUES THAT YOU EXPERIENCE DUE TO THE EFFECTS OF RSD ON YOUR PSYCHE.

VALIDATE YOUR FEELINGS EVERY DAY, SET BOUNDARIES TO MAINTAIN YOUR SELF-ESTEEM AND PROTECT YOURSELF FROM PSYCHOLOGICAL HARM, IN THE MEDIUM TERM, CREATE A SUPPORT NETWORK OF VERY TRUSTED FRIENDS AND SHOW ON THIS SHEET HOW THIS WILL HELP YOU AND WRITE DOWN THEIR CONTRIBUTIONS AND ENCOURAGEMENT TO DEAL WITH RSD, DON'T FORGET TO PRACTICE DAILY SELF-COMPASSION AFFIRMATIONS, WRITE DOWN YOUR CORE VALUES AND HOW YOU PRIORITIZE YOUR PSYCHOLOGICAL AND EMOTIONAL NEEDS.
DON'T FORGET TO CELEBRATE YOUR PROGRESS ALONG THE WAY AND YOUR DAILY VICTORIES AGAINST RSD!

_____

_____

_____

_____

_____

_____

_____

_____

_____

_____

_____

_____

_____

_____

_____

_____

_____

# RSD-ADHD
# OPPOSITE ACTION PLAN WORKSHEET

*THIS WORKSHEET IS INTENDED TO HELP YOU ACT AGAINST UNHELPFUL EMOTIONAL URGES, ESPECIALLY THOSE THAT MAY LEAD TO ISOLATION, AVOIDANCE, OR IMPULSIVE BEHAVIORS. DIRECTIONS: WHEN YOU FEEL A STRONG EMOTION (ESPECIALLY AN ADHD-RELATED EMOTION SUCH AS REJECTION), IDENTIFY AN OPPOSING ACTION—SOMETHING THAT HELPS BALANCE THE URGE. FOLLOW THE PLAN BELOW.*

| Emotions | Emotion Urge (What do you want to do?) | Opposite Action (What can you do instead?) | How Do You Feel After? |
|---|---|---|---|
|  |  |  |  |
|  |  |  |  |
|  |  |  |  |
|  |  |  |  |
|  |  |  |  |
|  |  |  |  |

# RSD
## INTERACTIONS WORKSHEET

START YOUR DAY WITH A POSITIVE AFFIRMATION AND TACKLE A SMALL, SIMPLE TASK TO GIVE YOURSELF A QUICK SENSE OF ACCOMPLISHMENT. BREAK LARGER TASKS INTO MANAGEABLE STEPS AND SET TIMERS FOR FOCUSED WORK, TAKING SHORT BREAKS IN BETWEEN TO AVOID FEELING OVERWHELMED. REGULARLY CHECK IN WITH YOUR EMOTIONS, ESPECIALLY AFTER TASKS, AND BE KIND TO YOURSELF IF FEELINGS OF REJECTION OR FRUSTRATION ARISE—IT'S OKAY TO FEEL THOSE THINGS. ACKNOWLEDGE ANY CHALLENGES, AND END THE DAY WITH A POSITIVE AFFIRMATION.

✓ ___ : ___

✓ ___ : ___

**THINGS TO WORK ON**

Sleep Quality:

## MOOD TRACKER ✓

- ANGRY ☐
- UPSET ☐
- ANXIOUS ☐
- EMBARRASSED ☐
- UNCOMFORTABLE ☐
- BRAVE ☐
- CALM ☐
- JOYFUL ☐
- PEACEFUL ☐
- CONFUSED ☐
- DISCOURAGED ☐
- DISTRACTED ☐
- EMBARRASSED ☐
- EXCITED ☐
- FRIENDLY ☐
- GUILTY ☐
- HAPPY ☐
- HOPEFUL ☐
- LONELY ☐
- LOVED ☐
- NERVOUS ☐
- OFFENDED ☐
- SCARED ☐
- THOUGHTFUL ☐
- TIRED ☐
- UNCOMFORTABLE ☐
- INSECURE ☐

# OVERCOMING RSD
# PRACTICAL WORKSHEET

Engage in a social situation that you think will enhance your RSD symptoms. Try to interact in a healthy way and remain in control of your feelings outwardly without withdrawing or getting angry. Maintain your self-respect and faith in yourself in situations that require this.

Be bold and engage in situations that reinforce your preconceived sense of failure. Gradually exposing and analyzing these situations enables you to get rid of psychological fragility, build your self-esteem, and gain social intelligence.

| WRITE THE MOST IMPORTANT DETAILS OF THE SITUATION IN THE CORRESPONDING BOX. | EVALUATE YOUR REACTIONS AND INTERACTIONS. (GOOD DEALING AND BAD DEALING) |
|---|---|
| | 👍 |
| | 🖐 |

DATE :        /        /

## EXPOSURE THERAPY
## FOR RSD TRAITS

Before engaging in social situations that might trigger RSD, take a moment to plan how you will handle potential emotional triggers. You may want to remind yourself that every comment or interaction is not a reflection of your worth, and that it's okay to step back if you start to feel overwhelmed. Visualizing how you would react to certain situations can help reduce anxiety and give you a sense of control. After the event, use the second part of the chart to assess how well you managed your emotional responses to perceived rejection or criticism, and to assess your level of control over any triggers.

*WHAT SHOULD I DO :*

| | |
|---|---|
| | Evaluating my success rate in controlling feelings of rejection or criticism  ○ ○ ○ ○ ○ |
| | Evaluating my success rate in showing balance and self-respect  ○ ○ ○ ○ ○ |
| | Evaluating my success rate in avoiding false perfection to avoid failure  ○ ○ ○ ○ ○ |

## NOTES

# RSD DIALECTICAL WORKSHEET

Date

CHALLENGE AND CORRECT NEGATIVE BEHAVIOR PATTERNS AND THOUGHTS

ON THIS WORKSHEET, START THINKING ABOUT YOUR TRIGGERS FOR ANXIETY, EXCESSIVE SHYNESS, REJECTION SENSITIVITY, AND CONFLICTING VALUES THAT YOU EXPERIENCE DUE TO THE EFFECTS OF RSD ON YOUR PSYCHE.

VALIDATE YOUR FEELINGS EVERY DAY, SET BOUNDARIES TO MAINTAIN YOUR SELF-ESTEEM AND PROTECT YOURSELF FROM PSYCHOLOGICAL HARM, IN THE MEDIUM TERM, CREATE A SUPPORT NETWORK OF VERY TRUSTED FRIENDS AND SHOW ON THIS SHEET HOW THIS WILL HELP YOU AND WRITE DOWN THEIR CONTRIBUTIONS AND ENCOURAGEMENT TO DEAL WITH RSD, DON'T FORGET TO PRACTICE DAILY SELF-COMPASSION AFFIRMATIONS, WRITE DOWN YOUR CORE VALUES AND HOW YOU PRIORITIZE YOUR PSYCHOLOGICAL AND EMOTIONAL NEEDS.
DON'T FORGET TO CELEBRATE YOUR PROGRESS ALONG THE WAY AND YOUR DAILY VICTORIES AGAINST RSD!

# RSD-ADHD
# OPPOSITE ACTION PLAN WORKSHEET

*THIS WORKSHEET IS INTENDED TO HELP YOU ACT AGAINST UNHELPFUL EMOTIONAL URGES, ESPECIALLY THOSE THAT MAY LEAD TO ISOLATION, AVOIDANCE, OR IMPULSIVE BEHAVIORS. DIRECTIONS: WHEN YOU FEEL A STRONG EMOTION (ESPECIALLY AN ADHD-RELATED EMOTION SUCH AS REJECTION), IDENTIFY AN OPPOSING ACTION—SOMETHING THAT HELPS BALANCE THE URGE. FOLLOW THE PLAN BELOW.*

| Emotions | Emotion Urge (What do you want to do?) | Opposite Action (What can you do instead?) | How Do You Feel After? |
|---|---|---|---|
| | | | |
| | | | |
| | | | |
| | | | |
| | | | |
| | | | |

# RSD
# INTERACTIONS WORKSHEET

START YOUR DAY WITH A POSITIVE AFFIRMATION AND TACKLE A SMALL, SIMPLE TASK TO GIVE YOURSELF A QUICK SENSE OF ACCOMPLISHMENT. BREAK LARGER TASKS INTO MANAGEABLE STEPS AND SET TIMERS FOR FOCUSED WORK, TAKING SHORT BREAKS IN BETWEEN TO AVOID FEELING OVERWHELMED. REGULARLY CHECK IN WITH YOUR EMOTIONS, ESPECIALLY AFTER TASKS, AND BE KIND TO YOURSELF IF FEELINGS OF REJECTION OR FRUSTRATION ARISE—IT'S OKAY TO FEEL THOSE THINGS. ACKNOWLEDGE ANY CHALLENGES, AND END THE DAY WITH A POSITIVE AFFIRMATION.

Sleep Quality:

## MOOD TRACKER

| Mood | ✓ |
|---|---|
| ANGRY | ☐ |
| UPSET | ☐ |
| ANXIOUS | ☐ |
| EMBARRASSED | ☐ |
| UNCOMFORTABLE | ☐ |
| BRAVE | ☐ |
| CALM | ☐ |
| JOYFUL | ☐ |
| PEACEFUL | ☐ |
| CONFUSED | ☐ |
| DISCOURAGED | ☐ |
| DISTRACTED | ☐ |
| EMBARRASSED | ☐ |
| EXCITED | ☐ |
| FRIENDLY | ☐ |
| GUILTY | ☐ |
| HAPPY | ☐ |
| HOPEFUL | ☐ |
| LONELY | ☐ |
| LOVED | ☐ |
| NERVOUS | ☐ |
| OFFENDED | ☐ |
| SCARED | ☐ |
| THOUGHTFUL | ☐ |
| TIRED | ☐ |
| UNCOMFORTABLE | ☐ |
| INSECURE | ☐ |

THINGS TO WORK ON

# OVERCOMING RSD
# PRACTICAL WORKSHEET

Engage in a social situation that you think will enhance your RSD symptoms. Try to interact in a healthy way and remain in control of your feelings outwardly without withdrawing or getting angry. Maintain your self-respect and faith in yourself in situations that require this.

Be bold and engage in situations that reinforce your preconceived sense of failure. Gradually exposing and analyzing these situations enables you to get rid of psychological fragility, build your self-esteem, and gain social intelligence.

| WRITE THE MOST IMPORTANT DETAILS OF THE SITUATION IN THE CORRESPONDING BOX. | EVALUATE YOUR REACTIONS AND INTERACTIONS. (GOOD DEALING AND BAD DEALING) |
|---|---|
| | 👍 |
| | 🖐 |

DATE :          /          /

# EXPOSURE THERAPY
# FOR RSD TRAITS

Before engaging in social situations that might trigger RSD, take a moment to plan how you will handle potential emotional triggers. You may want to remind yourself that every comment or interaction is not a reflection of your worth, and that it's okay to step back if you start to feel overwhelmed. Visualizing how you would react to certain situations can help reduce anxiety and give you a sense of control. After the event, use the second part of the chart to assess how well you managed your emotional responses to perceived rejection or criticism, and to assess your level of control over any triggers.

*WHAT SHOULD I DO :*

| | Evaluating my success rate in controlling feelings of rejection or criticism ○ ○ ○ ○ ○ |
| --- | --- |
| | Evaluating my success rate in showing balance and self-respect ○ ○ ○ ○ ○ |
| | Evaluating my success rate in avoiding false perfection to avoid failure ○ ○ ○ ○ ○ |

# NOTES

# RSD DIALECTICAL WORKSHEET

CHALLENGE AND CORRECT NEGATIVE BEHAVIOR PATTERNS
AND THOUGHTS

ON THIS WORKSHEET, START THINKING ABOUT YOUR TRIGGERS FOR ANXIETY, EXCESSIVE SHYNESS, REJECTION SENSITIVITY, AND CONFLICTING VALUES THAT YOU EXPERIENCE DUE TO THE EFFECTS OF RSD ON YOUR PSYCHE.

VALIDATE YOUR FEELINGS EVERY DAY, SET BOUNDARIES TO MAINTAIN YOUR SELF-ESTEEM AND PROTECT YOURSELF FROM PSYCHOLOGICAL HARM, IN THE MEDIUM TERM, CREATE A SUPPORT NETWORK OF VERY TRUSTED FRIENDS AND SHOW ON THIS SHEET HOW THIS WILL HELP YOU AND WRITE DOWN THEIR CONTRIBUTIONS AND ENCOURAGEMENT TO DEAL WITH RSD, DON'T FORGET TO PRACTICE DAILY SELF-COMPASSION AFFIRMATIONS, WRITE DOWN YOUR CORE VALUES AND HOW YOU PRIORITIZE YOUR PSYCHOLOGICAL AND EMOTIONAL NEEDS.
DON'T FORGET TO CELEBRATE YOUR PROGRESS ALONG THE WAY AND YOUR DAILY VICTORIES AGAINST RSD!

# RSD-ADHD
# OPPOSITE ACTION PLAN WORKSHEET

THIS WORKSHEET IS INTENDED TO HELP YOU ACT AGAINST UNHELPFUL EMOTIONAL URGES, ESPECIALLY THOSE THAT MAY LEAD TO ISOLATION, AVOIDANCE, OR IMPULSIVE BEHAVIORS. DIRECTIONS: WHEN YOU FEEL A STRONG EMOTION (ESPECIALLY AN ADHD-RELATED EMOTION SUCH AS REJECTION), IDENTIFY AN OPPOSING ACTION—SOMETHING THAT HELPS BALANCE THE URGE. FOLLOW THE PLAN BELOW.

| Emotions | Emotion Urge (What do you want to do?) | Opposite Action (What can you do instead?) | How Do You Feel After? |
|---|---|---|---|
|  |  |  |  |
|  |  |  |  |
|  |  |  |  |
|  |  |  |  |
|  |  |  |  |
|  |  |  |  |

# RSD
# INTERACTIONS WORKSHEET

START YOUR DAY WITH A POSITIVE AFFIRMATION AND TACKLE A SMALL, SIMPLE TASK TO GIVE YOURSELF A QUICK SENSE OF ACCOMPLISHMENT. BREAK LARGER TASKS INTO MANAGEABLE STEPS AND SET TIMERS FOR FOCUSED WORK, TAKING SHORT BREAKS IN BETWEEN TO AVOID FEELING OVERWHELMED. REGULARLY CHECK IN WITH YOUR EMOTIONS, ESPECIALLY AFTER TASKS, AND BE KIND TO YOURSELF IF FEELINGS OF REJECTION OR FRUSTRATION ARISE—IT'S OKAY TO FEEL THOSE THINGS. ACKNOWLEDGE ANY CHALLENGES, AND END THE DAY WITH A POSITIVE AFFIRMATION.

✓ ___ : ___

✓ ___ : ___

## THINGS TO WORK ON

## MOOD TRACKER ✓

- ANGRY ☐
- UPSET ☐
- ANXIOUS ☐
- EMBARRASSED ☐
- UNCOMFORTABLE ☐
- BRAVE ☐
- CALM ☐
- JOYFUL ☐
- PEACEFUL ☐
- CONFUSED ☐
- DISCOURAGED ☐
- DISTRACTED ☐
- EMBARRASSED ☐
- EXCITED ☐
- FRIENDLY ☐
- GUILTY ☐
- HAPPY ☐
- HOPEFUL ☐
- LONELY ☐
- LOVED ☐
- NERVOUS ☐
- OFFENDED ☐
- SCARED ☐
- THOUGHTFUL ☐
- TIRED ☐
- UNCOMFORTABLE ☐
- INSECURE ☐

# OVERCOMING RSD
# PRACTICAL WORKSHEET

Engage in a social situation that you think will enhance your RSD symptoms. Try to interact in a healthy way and remain in control of your feelings outwardly without withdrawing or getting angry. Maintain your self-respect and faith in yourself in situations that require this.

Be bold and engage in situations that reinforce your preconceived sense of failure. Gradually exposing and analyzing these situations enables you to get rid of psychological fragility, build your self-esteem, and gain social intelligence.

| WRITE THE MOST IMPORTANT DETAILS OF THE SITUATION IN THE CORRESPONDING BOX. | EVALUATE YOUR REACTIONS AND INTERACTIONS. (GOOD DEALING AND BAD DEALING) |
|---|---|
| | 👍 |
| | ✋ |

DATE :        /        /

## EXPOSURE THERAPY FOR RSD TRAITS

Before engaging in social situations that might trigger RSD, take a moment to plan how you will handle potential emotional triggers. You may want to remind yourself that every comment or interaction is not a reflection of your worth, and that it's okay to step back if you start to feel overwhelmed. Visualizing how you would react to certain situations can help reduce anxiety and give you a sense of control. After the event, use the second part of the chart to assess how well you managed your emotional responses to perceived rejection or criticism, and to assess your level of control over any triggers.

*WHAT SHOULD I DO :*

|  | Evaluating my success rate in controlling feelings of rejection or criticism<br>○ ○ ○ ○ ○ |
|---|---|
|  | Evaluating my success rate in showing balance and self-respect<br>○ ○ ○ ○ ○ |
|  | Evaluating my success rate in avoiding false perfection to avoid failure<br>○ ○ ○ ○ ○ |

## NOTES

# RSD DIALECTICAL WORKSHEET

CHALLENGE AND CORRECT NEGATIVE BEHAVIOR PATTERNS
AND THOUGHTS

ON THIS WORKSHEET, START THINKING ABOUT YOUR TRIGGERS FOR ANXIETY, EXCESSIVE SHYNESS, REJECTION SENSITIVITY, AND CONFLICTING VALUES THAT YOU EXPERIENCE DUE TO THE EFFECTS OF RSD ON YOUR PSYCHE.

VALIDATE YOUR FEELINGS EVERY DAY, SET BOUNDARIES TO MAINTAIN YOUR SELF-ESTEEM AND PROTECT YOURSELF FROM PSYCHOLOGICAL HARM, IN THE MEDIUM TERM, CREATE A SUPPORT NETWORK OF VERY TRUSTED FRIENDS AND SHOW ON THIS SHEET HOW THIS WILL HELP YOU AND WRITE DOWN THEIR CONTRIBUTIONS AND ENCOURAGEMENT TO DEAL WITH RSD, DON'T FORGET TO PRACTICE DAILY SELF-COMPASSION AFFIRMATIONS, WRITE DOWN YOUR CORE VALUES AND HOW YOU PRIORITIZE YOUR PSYCHOLOGICAL AND EMOTIONAL NEEDS.
DON'T FORGET TO CELEBRATE YOUR PROGRESS ALONG THE WAY AND YOUR DAILY VICTORIES AGAINST RSD!

THIS WORKSHEET IS INTENDED TO HELP YOU ACT AGAINST UNHELPFUL EMOTIONAL URGES, ESPECIALLY THOSE THAT MAY LEAD TO ISOLATION, AVOIDANCE, OR IMPULSIVE BEHAVIORS. DIRECTIONS: WHEN YOU FEEL A STRONG EMOTION (ESPECIALLY AN ADHD-RELATED EMOTION SUCH AS REJECTION), IDENTIFY AN OPPOSING ACTION—SOMETHING THAT HELPS BALANCE THE URGE. FOLLOW THE PLAN BELOW.

| Emotions | Emotion Urge (What do you want to do?) | Opposite Action (What can you do instead?) | How Do You Feel After? |
|---|---|---|---|
|  |  |  |  |
|  |  |  |  |
|  |  |  |  |
|  |  |  |  |
|  |  |  |  |
|  |  |  |  |

# RSD
# INTERACTIONS WORKSHEET

START YOUR DAY WITH A POSITIVE AFFIRMATION AND TACKLE A SMALL, SIMPLE TASK TO GIVE YOURSELF A QUICK SENSE OF ACCOMPLISHMENT. BREAK LARGER TASKS INTO MANAGEABLE STEPS AND SET TIMERS FOR FOCUSED WORK, TAKING SHORT BREAKS IN BETWEEN TO AVOID FEELING OVERWHELMED. REGULARLY CHECK IN WITH YOUR EMOTIONS, ESPECIALLY AFTER TASKS, AND BE KIND TO YOURSELF IF FEELINGS OF REJECTION OR FRUSTRATION ARISE—IT'S OKAY TO FEEL THOSE THINGS. ACKNOWLEDGE ANY CHALLENGES, AND END THE DAY WITH A POSITIVE AFFIRMATION.

⊘ ___ : ___

⊘ ___ : ___

## THINGS TO WORK ON

Sleep Quality:

## MOOD TRACKER ✓

| | |
|---|---|
| ANGRY | ☐ |
| UPSET | ☐ |
| ANXIOUS | ☐ |
| EMBARRASSED | ☐ |
| UNCOMFORTABLE | ☐ |
| BRAVE | ☐ |
| CALM | ☐ |
| JOYFUL | ☐ |
| PEACEFUL | ☐ |
| CONFUSED | ☐ |
| DISCOURAGED | ☐ |
| DISTRACTED | ☐ |
| EMBARRASSED | ☐ |
| EXCITED | ☐ |
| FRIENDLY | ☐ |
| GUILTY | ☐ |
| HAPPY | ☐ |
| HOPEFUL | ☐ |
| LONELY | ☐ |
| LOVED | ☐ |
| NERVOUS | ☐ |
| OFFENDED | ☐ |
| SCARED | ☐ |
| THOUGHTFUL | ☐ |
| TIRED | ☐ |
| UNCOMFORTABLE | ☐ |
| INSECURE | ☐ |

# OVERCOMING RSD
# PRACTICAL WORKSHEET

Engage in a social situation that you think will enhance your RSD symptoms. Try to interact in a healthy way and remain in control of your feelings outwardly without withdrawing or getting angry. Maintain your self-respect and faith in yourself in situations that require this.

Be bold and engage in situations that reinforce your preconceived sense of failure. Gradually exposing and analyzing these situations enables you to get rid of psychological fragility, build your self-esteem, and gain social intelligence.

| WRITE THE MOST IMPORTANT DETAILS OF THE SITUATION IN THE CORRESPONDING BOX. | EVALUATE YOUR REACTIONS AND INTERACTIONS. (GOOD DEALING AND BAD DEALING) |
|---|---|
| | 👍 |
| | ✋ |

DATE :        /        /

# EXPOSURE THERAPY
# FOR RSD TRAITS

Before engaging in social situations that might trigger RSD, take a moment to plan how you will handle potential emotional triggers. You may want to remind yourself that every comment or interaction is not a reflection of your worth, and that it's okay to step back if you start to feel overwhelmed. Visualizing how you would react to certain situations can help reduce anxiety and give you a sense of control. After the event, use the second part of the chart to assess how well you managed your emotional responses to perceived rejection or criticism, and to assess your level of control over any triggers.

*WHAT SHOULD I DO :*

| | |
|---|---|
| | Evaluating my success rate in controlling feelings of rejection or criticism<br><br>○ ○ ○ ○ ○ |
| | Evaluating my success rate in showing balance and self-respect<br><br>○ ○ ○ ○ ○ |
| | Evaluating my success rate in avoiding false perfection to avoid failure<br><br>○ ○ ○ ○ ○ |

# NOTES

# RSD DIALECTICAL WORKSHEET

CHALLENGE AND CORRECT NEGATIVE BEHAVIOR PATTERNS
AND THOUGHTS

ON THIS WORKSHEET, START THINKING ABOUT YOUR TRIGGERS FOR ANXIETY, EXCESSIVE SHYNESS, REJECTION SENSITIVITY, AND CONFLICTING VALUES THAT YOU EXPERIENCE DUE TO THE EFFECTS OF RSD ON YOUR PSYCHE.

VALIDATE YOUR FEELINGS EVERY DAY, SET BOUNDARIES TO MAINTAIN YOUR SELF-ESTEEM AND PROTECT YOURSELF FROM PSYCHOLOGICAL HARM, IN THE MEDIUM TERM, CREATE A SUPPORT NETWORK OF VERY TRUSTED FRIENDS AND SHOW ON THIS SHEET HOW THIS WILL HELP YOU AND WRITE DOWN THEIR CONTRIBUTIONS AND ENCOURAGEMENT TO DEAL WITH RSD, DON'T FORGET TO PRACTICE DAILY SELF-COMPASSION AFFIRMATIONS, WRITE DOWN YOUR CORE VALUES AND HOW YOU PRIORITIZE YOUR PSYCHOLOGICAL AND EMOTIONAL NEEDS.
DON'T FORGET TO CELEBRATE YOUR PROGRESS ALONG THE WAY AND YOUR DAILY VICTORIES AGAINST RSD!

_____

_____

_____

_____

_____

_____

_____

_____

_____

_____

_____

_____

_____

_____

_____

_____

_____

# RSD-ADHD
## OPPOSITE ACTION PLAN WORKSHEET

*THIS WORKSHEET IS INTENDED TO HELP YOU ACT AGAINST UNHELPFUL EMOTIONAL URGES, ESPECIALLY THOSE THAT MAY LEAD TO ISOLATION, AVOIDANCE, OR IMPULSIVE BEHAVIORS. DIRECTIONS: WHEN YOU FEEL A STRONG EMOTION (ESPECIALLY AN ADHD-RELATED EMOTION SUCH AS REJECTION), IDENTIFY AN OPPOSING ACTION—SOMETHING THAT HELPS BALANCE THE URGE. FOLLOW THE PLAN BELOW.*

| Emotions | Emotion Urge (What do you want to do?) | Opposite Action (What can you do instead?) | How Do You Feel After? |
|---|---|---|---|
|  |  |  |  |
|  |  |  |  |
|  |  |  |  |
|  |  |  |  |
|  |  |  |  |
|  |  |  |  |

# RSD
# INTERACTIONS WORKSHEET

START YOUR DAY WITH A POSITIVE AFFIRMATION AND TACKLE A SMALL, SIMPLE TASK TO GIVE YOURSELF A QUICK SENSE OF ACCOMPLISHMENT. BREAK LARGER TASKS INTO MANAGEABLE STEPS AND SET TIMERS FOR FOCUSED WORK, TAKING SHORT BREAKS IN BETWEEN TO AVOID FEELING OVERWHELMED. REGULARLY CHECK IN WITH YOUR EMOTIONS, ESPECIALLY AFTER TASKS, AND BE KIND TO YOURSELF IF FEELINGS OF REJECTION OR FRUSTRATION ARISE—IT'S OKAY TO FEEL THOSE THINGS. ACKNOWLEDGE ANY CHALLENGES, AND END THE DAY WITH A POSITIVE AFFIRMATION.

⊘ ___ : ___

⊘ ___ : ___

## THINGS TO WORK ON

## MOOD TRACKER ✓

| | |
|---|---|
| ANGRY | ☐ |
| UPSET | ☐ |
| ANXIOUS | ☐ |
| EMBARRASSED | ☐ |
| UNCOMFORTABLE | ☐ |
| BRAVE | ☐ |
| CALM | ☐ |
| JOYFUL | ☐ |
| PEACEFUL | ☐ |
| CONFUSED | ☐ |
| DISCOURAGED | ☐ |
| DISTRACTED | ☐ |
| EMBARRASSED | ☐ |
| EXCITED | ☐ |
| FRIENDLY | ☐ |
| GUILTY | ☐ |
| HAPPY | ☐ |
| HOPEFUL | ☐ |
| LONELY | ☐ |
| LOVED | ☐ |
| NERVOUS | ☐ |
| OFFENDED | ☐ |
| SCARED | ☐ |
| THOUGHTFUL | ☐ |
| TIRED | ☐ |
| UNCOMFORTABLE | ☐ |
| INSECURE | ☐ |

# OVERCOMING RSD
# PRACTICAL WORKSHEET

Engage in a social situation that you think will enhance your RSD symptoms. Try to interact in a healthy way and remain in control of your feelings outwardly without withdrawing or getting angry. Maintain your self-respect and faith in yourself in situations that require this.
Be bold and engage in situations that reinforce your preconceived sense of failure. Gradually exposing and analyzing these situations enables you to get rid of psychological fragility, build your self-esteem, and gain social intelligence.

| WRITE THE MOST IMPORTANT DETAILS OF THE SITUATION IN THE CORRESPONDING BOX. | EVALUATE YOUR REACTIONS AND INTERACTIONS. (GOOD DEALING AND BAD DEALING) |
|---|---|
| | 👍 |
| | 🖐 |

DATE :        /        /

## EXPOSURE THERAPY
## FOR RSD TRAITS

Before engaging in social situations that might trigger RSD, take a moment to plan how you will handle potential emotional triggers. You may want to remind yourself that every comment or interaction is not a reflection of your worth, and that it's okay to step back if you start to feel overwhelmed. Visualizing how you would react to certain situations can help reduce anxiety and give you a sense of control. After the event, use the second part of the chart to assess how well you managed your emotional responses to perceived rejection or criticism, and to assess your level of control over any triggers.

*WHAT SHOULD I DO :*

| | |
|---|---|
| | Evaluating my success rate in controlling feelings of rejection or criticism<br>○ ○ ○ ○ ○ |
| | Evaluating my success rate in showing balance and self-respect<br>○ ○ ○ ○ ○ |
| | Evaluating my success rate in avoiding false perfection to avoid failure<br>○ ○ ○ ○ ○ |

## NOTES

# RSD DIALECTICAL WORKSHEET

CHALLENGE AND CORRECT NEGATIVE BEHAVIOR PATTERNS
AND THOUGHTS

ON THIS WORKSHEET, START THINKING ABOUT YOUR TRIGGERS FOR ANXIETY, EXCESSIVE SHYNESS, REJECTION SENSITIVITY, AND CONFLICTING VALUES THAT YOU EXPERIENCE DUE TO THE EFFECTS OF RSD ON YOUR PSYCHE.

VALIDATE YOUR FEELINGS EVERY DAY, SET BOUNDARIES TO MAINTAIN YOUR SELF-ESTEEM AND PROTECT YOURSELF FROM PSYCHOLOGICAL HARM, IN THE MEDIUM TERM, CREATE A SUPPORT NETWORK OF VERY TRUSTED FRIENDS AND SHOW ON THIS SHEET HOW THIS WILL HELP YOU AND WRITE DOWN THEIR CONTRIBUTIONS AND ENCOURAGEMENT TO DEAL WITH RSD, DON'T FORGET TO PRACTICE DAILY SELF-COMPASSION AFFIRMATIONS, WRITE DOWN YOUR CORE VALUES AND HOW YOU PRIORITIZE YOUR PSYCHOLOGICAL AND EMOTIONAL NEEDS.
DON'T FORGET TO CELEBRATE YOUR PROGRESS ALONG THE WAY AND YOUR DAILY VICTORIES AGAINST RSD!

# RSD-ADHD
## OPPOSITE ACTION PLAN WORKSHEET

THIS WORKSHEET IS INTENDED TO HELP YOU ACT AGAINST
UNHELPFUL EMOTIONAL URGES, ESPECIALLY THOSE THAT MAY LEAD
TO ISOLATION, AVOIDANCE, OR IMPULSIVE BEHAVIORS.
DIRECTIONS: WHEN YOU FEEL A STRONG EMOTION (ESPECIALLY AN
ADHD-RELATED EMOTION SUCH AS REJECTION), IDENTIFY AN
OPPOSING ACTION—SOMETHING THAT HELPS BALANCE THE URGE.
FOLLOW THE PLAN BELOW.

| Emotions | Emotion Urge (What do you want to do?) | Opposite Action (What can you do instead?) | How Do You Feel After? |
|---|---|---|---|
|  |  |  |  |
|  |  |  |  |
|  |  |  |  |
|  |  |  |  |
|  |  |  |  |
|  |  |  |  |

# RSD
# INTERACTIONS WORKSHEET

START YOUR DAY WITH A POSITIVE AFFIRMATION AND TACKLE A SMALL, SIMPLE TASK TO GIVE YOURSELF A QUICK SENSE OF ACCOMPLISHMENT. BREAK LARGER TASKS INTO MANAGEABLE STEPS AND SET TIMERS FOR FOCUSED WORK, TAKING SHORT BREAKS IN BETWEEN TO AVOID FEELING OVERWHELMED. REGULARLY CHECK IN WITH YOUR EMOTIONS, ESPECIALLY AFTER TASKS, AND BE KIND TO YOURSELF IF FEELINGS OF REJECTION OR FRUSTRATION ARISE—IT'S OKAY TO FEEL THOSE THINGS. ACKNOWLEDGE ANY CHALLENGES, AND END THE DAY WITH A POSITIVE AFFIRMATION.

Sleep Quality:

## MOOD TRACKER ✔

| | |
|---|---|
| ANGRY | ☐ |
| UPSET | ☐ |
| ANXIOUS | ☐ |
| EMBARRASSED | ☐ |
| UNCOMFORTABLE | ☐ |
| BRAVE | ☐ |
| CALM | ☐ |
| JOYFUL | ☐ |
| PEACEFUL | ☐ |
| CONFUSED | ☐ |
| DISCOURAGED | ☐ |
| DISTRACTED | ☐ |
| EMBARRASSED | ☐ |
| EXCITED | ☐ |
| FRIENDLY | ☐ |
| GUILTY | ☐ |
| HAPPY | ☐ |
| HOPEFUL | ☐ |
| LONELY | ☐ |
| LOVED | ☐ |
| NERVOUS | ☐ |
| OFFENDED | ☐ |
| SCARED | ☐ |
| THOUGHTFUL | ☐ |
| TIRED | ☐ |
| UNCOMFORTABLE | ☐ |
| INSECURE | ☐ |

⊘ ___ : ___

⊘ ___ : ___

## THINGS TO WORK ON

# OVERCOMING RSD
# PRACTICAL WORKSHEET

Engage in a social situation that you think will enhance your RSD symptoms. Try to interact in a healthy way and remain in control of your feelings outwardly without withdrawing or getting angry. Maintain your self-respect and faith in yourself in situations that require this.

Be bold and engage in situations that reinforce your preconceived sense of failure. Gradually exposing and analyzing these situations enables you to get rid of psychological fragility, build your self-esteem, and gain social intelligence.

| WRITE THE MOST IMPORTANT DETAILS OF THE SITUATION IN THE CORRESPONDING BOX. | EVALUATE YOUR REACTIONS AND INTERACTIONS. (GOOD DEALING AND BAD DEALING) |
|---|---|
| | |

DATE :        /        /

# EXPOSURE THERAPY
# FOR RSD TRAITS

Before engaging in social situations that might trigger RSD, take a moment to plan how you will handle potential emotional triggers. You may want to remind yourself that every comment or interaction is not a reflection of your worth, and that it's okay to step back if you start to feel overwhelmed. Visualizing how you would react to certain situations can help reduce anxiety and give you a sense of control. After the event, use the second part of the chart to assess how well you managed your emotional responses to perceived rejection or criticism, and to assess your level of control over any triggers.

*WHAT SHOULD I DO :*

| | |
|---|---|
| | Evaluating my success rate in controlling feelings of rejection or criticism<br>○ ○ ○ ○ ○ |
| | Evaluating my success rate in showing balance and self-respect<br>○ ○ ○ ○ ○ |
| | Evaluating my success rate in avoiding false perfection to avoid failure<br>○ ○ ○ ○ ○ |

# NOTES

# RSD DIALECTICAL WORKSHEET

*Date* ..............................................

CHALLENGE AND CORRECT NEGATIVE BEHAVIOR PATTERNS
AND THOUGHTS

ON THIS WORKSHEET, START THINKING ABOUT YOUR TRIGGERS FOR ANXIETY, EXCESSIVE SHYNESS, REJECTION SENSITIVITY, AND CONFLICTING VALUES THAT YOU EXPERIENCE DUE TO THE EFFECTS OF RSD ON YOUR PSYCHE.

VALIDATE YOUR FEELINGS EVERY DAY, SET BOUNDARIES TO MAINTAIN YOUR SELF-ESTEEM AND PROTECT YOURSELF FROM PSYCHOLOGICAL HARM, IN THE MEDIUM TERM, CREATE A SUPPORT NETWORK OF VERY TRUSTED FRIENDS AND SHOW ON THIS SHEET HOW THIS WILL HELP YOU AND WRITE DOWN THEIR CONTRIBUTIONS AND ENCOURAGEMENT TO DEAL WITH RSD, DON'T FORGET TO PRACTICE DAILY SELF-COMPASSION AFFIRMATIONS, WRITE DOWN YOUR CORE VALUES AND HOW YOU PRIORITIZE YOUR PSYCHOLOGICAL AND EMOTIONAL NEEDS.
DON'T FORGET TO CELEBRATE YOUR PROGRESS ALONG THE WAY AND YOUR DAILY VICTORIES AGAINST RSD!

_____

_____

_____

_____

_____

_____

_____

_____

_____

_____

_____

_____

_____

_____

_____

# RSD-ADHD
# OPPOSITE ACTION PLAN WORKSHEET

THIS WORKSHEET IS INTENDED TO HELP YOU ACT AGAINST UNHELPFUL EMOTIONAL URGES, ESPECIALLY THOSE THAT MAY LEAD TO ISOLATION, AVOIDANCE, OR IMPULSIVE BEHAVIORS. DIRECTIONS: WHEN YOU FEEL A STRONG EMOTION (ESPECIALLY AN ADHD-RELATED EMOTION SUCH AS REJECTION), IDENTIFY AN OPPOSING ACTION—SOMETHING THAT HELPS BALANCE THE URGE. FOLLOW THE PLAN BELOW.

| Emotions | Emotion Urge (What do you want to do?) | Opposite Action (What can you do instead?) | How Do You Feel After? |
|---|---|---|---|
|  |  |  |  |
|  |  |  |  |
|  |  |  |  |
|  |  |  |  |
|  |  |  |  |
|  |  |  |  |

# RSD
# INTERACTIONS WORKSHEET

START YOUR DAY WITH A POSITIVE AFFIRMATION AND TACKLE A SMALL, SIMPLE TASK TO GIVE YOURSELF A QUICK SENSE OF ACCOMPLISHMENT. BREAK LARGER TASKS INTO MANAGEABLE STEPS AND SET TIMERS FOR FOCUSED WORK, TAKING SHORT BREAKS IN BETWEEN TO AVOID FEELING OVERWHELMED. REGULARLY CHECK IN WITH YOUR EMOTIONS, ESPECIALLY AFTER TASKS, AND BE KIND TO YOURSELF IF FEELINGS OF REJECTION OR FRUSTRATION ARISE—IT'S OKAY TO FEEL THOSE THINGS. ACKNOWLEDGE ANY CHALLENGES, AND END THE DAY WITH A POSITIVE AFFIRMATION.

✓ ___ : ___

✓ ___ : ___

**THINGS TO WORK ON**

Sleep Quality:

## MOOD TRACKER ✓

| | |
|---|---|
| ANGRY | ☐ |
| UPSET | ☐ |
| ANXIOUS | ☐ |
| EMBARRASSED | ☐ |
| UNCOMFORTABLE | ☐ |
| BRAVE | ☐ |
| CALM | ☐ |
| JOYFUL | ☐ |
| PEACEFUL | ☐ |
| CONFUSED | ☐ |
| DISCOURAGED | ☐ |
| DISTRACTED | ☐ |
| EMBARRASSED | ☐ |
| EXCITED | ☐ |
| FRIENDLY | ☐ |
| GUILTY | ☐ |
| HAPPY | ☐ |
| HOPEFUL | ☐ |
| LONELY | ☐ |
| LOVED | ☐ |
| NERVOUS | ☐ |
| OFFENDED | ☐ |
| SCARED | ☐ |
| THOUGHTFUL | ☐ |
| TIRED | ☐ |
| UNCOMFORTABLE | ☐ |
| INSECURE | ☐ |

# OVERCOMING RSD
# PRACTICAL WORKSHEET

Engage in a social situation that you think will enhance your RSD symptoms. Try to interact in a healthy way and remain in control of your feelings outwardly without withdrawing or getting angry. Maintain your self-respect and faith in yourself in situations that require this.

Be bold and engage in situations that reinforce your preconceived sense of failure. Gradually exposing and analyzing these situations enables you to get rid of psychological fragility, build your self-esteem, and gain social intelligence.

| WRITE THE MOST IMPORTANT DETAILS OF THE SITUATION IN THE CORRESPONDING BOX. | EVALUATE YOUR REACTIONS AND INTERACTIONS. (GOOD DEALING AND BAD DEALING) |
|---|---|
| | 👍 |
| | 🖐 |

DATE :        /        /

## EXPOSURE THERAPY FOR RSD TRAITS

Before engaging in social situations that might trigger RSD, take a moment to plan how you will handle potential emotional triggers. You may want to remind yourself that every comment or interaction is not a reflection of your worth, and that it's okay to step back if you start to feel overwhelmed. Visualizing how you would react to certain situations can help reduce anxiety and give you a sense of control. After the event, use the second part of the chart to assess how well you managed your emotional responses to perceived rejection or criticism, and to assess your level of control over any triggers.

*WHAT SHOULD I DO :*

| | |
|---|---|
| | Evaluating my success rate in controlling feelings of rejection or criticism ○ ○ ○ ○ ○ |
| | Evaluating my success rate in showing balance and self-respect ○ ○ ○ ○ ○ |
| | Evaluating my success rate in avoiding false perfection to avoid failure ○ ○ ○ ○ ○ |

## NOTES

# RSD DIALECTICAL WORKSHEET

CHALLENGE AND CORRECT NEGATIVE BEHAVIOR PATTERNS
AND THOUGHTS

ON THIS WORKSHEET, START THINKING ABOUT YOUR TRIGGERS FOR ANXIETY, EXCESSIVE SHYNESS, REJECTION SENSITIVITY, AND CONFLICTING VALUES THAT YOU EXPERIENCE DUE TO THE EFFECTS OF RSD ON YOUR PSYCHE.

VALIDATE YOUR FEELINGS EVERY DAY, SET BOUNDARIES TO MAINTAIN YOUR SELF-ESTEEM AND PROTECT YOURSELF FROM PSYCHOLOGICAL HARM, IN THE MEDIUM TERM, CREATE A SUPPORT NETWORK OF VERY TRUSTED FRIENDS AND SHOW ON THIS SHEET HOW THIS WILL HELP YOU AND WRITE DOWN THEIR CONTRIBUTIONS AND ENCOURAGEMENT TO DEAL WITH RSD, DON'T FORGET TO PRACTICE DAILY SELF-COMPASSION AFFIRMATIONS, WRITE DOWN YOUR CORE VALUES AND HOW YOU PRIORITIZE YOUR PSYCHOLOGICAL AND EMOTIONAL NEEDS.
DON'T FORGET TO CELEBRATE YOUR PROGRESS ALONG THE WAY AND YOUR DAILY VICTORIES AGAINST RSD!

_____

_____

_____

_____

_____

_____

_____

_____

_____

_____

_____

_____

_____

_____

_____

_____

*THIS WORKSHEET IS INTENDED TO HELP YOU ACT AGAINST UNHELPFUL EMOTIONAL URGES, ESPECIALLY THOSE THAT MAY LEAD TO ISOLATION, AVOIDANCE, OR IMPULSIVE BEHAVIORS. DIRECTIONS: WHEN YOU FEEL A STRONG EMOTION (ESPECIALLY AN ADHD-RELATED EMOTION SUCH AS REJECTION), IDENTIFY AN OPPOSING ACTION—SOMETHING THAT HELPS BALANCE THE URGE. FOLLOW THE PLAN BELOW.*

| Emotions | Emotion Urge (What do you want to do?) | Opposite Action (What can you do instead?) | How Do You Feel After? |
|---|---|---|---|
|  |  |  |  |
|  |  |  |  |
|  |  |  |  |
|  |  |  |  |
|  |  |  |  |
|  |  |  |  |

# RSD
# INTERACTIONS WORKSHEET

START YOUR DAY WITH A POSITIVE AFFIRMATION AND TACKLE A SMALL, SIMPLE TASK TO GIVE YOURSELF A QUICK SENSE OF ACCOMPLISHMENT. BREAK LARGER TASKS INTO MANAGEABLE STEPS AND SET TIMERS FOR FOCUSED WORK, TAKING SHORT BREAKS IN BETWEEN TO AVOID FEELING OVERWHELMED. REGULARLY CHECK IN WITH YOUR EMOTIONS, ESPECIALLY AFTER TASKS, AND BE KIND TO YOURSELF IF FEELINGS OF REJECTION OR FRUSTRATION ARISE—IT'S OKAY TO FEEL THOSE THINGS. ACKNOWLEDGE ANY CHALLENGES, AND END THE DAY WITH A POSITIVE AFFIRMATION.

Date : / /

Sleep Quality:

## MOOD TRACKER ✓

| | |
|---|---|
| ANGRY | ☐ |
| UPSET | ☐ |
| ANXIOUS | ☐ |
| EMBARRASSED | ☐ |
| UNCOMFORTABLE | ☐ |
| BRAVE | ☐ |
| CALM | ☐ |
| JOYFUL | ☐ |
| PEACEFUL | ☐ |
| CONFUSED | ☐ |
| DISCOURAGED | ☐ |
| DISTRACTED | ☐ |
| EMBARRASSED | ☐ |
| EXCITED | ☐ |
| FRIENDLY | ☐ |
| GUILTY | ☐ |
| HAPPY | ☐ |
| HOPEFUL | ☐ |
| LONELY | ☐ |
| LOVED | ☐ |
| NERVOUS | ☐ |
| OFFENDED | ☐ |
| SCARED | ☐ |
| THOUGHTFUL | ☐ |
| TIRED | ☐ |
| UNCOMFORTABLE | ☐ |
| INSECURE | ☐ |

⊘ ___ : ___

⊘ ___ : ___

## THINGS TO WORK ON

# OVERCOMING RSD
# PRACTICAL WORKSHEET

Engage in a social situation that you think will enhance your RSD symptoms. Try to interact in a healthy way and remain in control of your feelings outwardly without withdrawing or getting angry. Maintain your self-respect and faith in yourself in situations that require this.

Be bold and engage in situations that reinforce your preconceived sense of failure. Gradually exposing and analyzing these situations enables you to get rid of psychological fragility, build your self-esteem, and gain social intelligence.

| WRITE THE MOST IMPORTANT DETAILS OF THE SITUATION IN THE CORRESPONDING BOX. | EVALUATE YOUR REACTIONS AND INTERACTIONS. (GOOD DEALING AND BAD DEALING) |
|---|---|
| | 👍 |
| | 🖐 |

DATE :        /        /

Before engaging in social situations that might trigger RSD, take a moment to plan how you will handle potential emotional triggers. You may want to remind yourself that every comment or interaction is not a reflection of your worth, and that it's okay to step back if you start to feel overwhelmed. Visualizing how you would react to certain situations can help reduce anxiety and give you a sense of control. After the event, use the second part of the chart to assess how well you managed your emotional responses to perceived rejection or criticism, and to assess your level of control over any triggers.

*WHAT SHOULD I DO :*

| | |
|---|---|
| | Evaluating my success rate in controlling feelings of rejection or criticism  ◯ ◯ ◯ ◯ ◯ |
| | Evaluating my success rate in showing balance and self-respect  ◯ ◯ ◯ ◯ ◯ |
| | Evaluating my success rate in avoiding false perfection to avoid failure  ◯ ◯ ◯ ◯ ◯ |

# NOTES

# RSD DIALECTICAL WORKSHEET

Date ...........................................

CHALLENGE AND CORRECT NEGATIVE BEHAVIOR PATTERNS
AND THOUGHTS

ON THIS WORKSHEET, START THINKING ABOUT YOUR TRIGGERS FOR ANXIETY, EXCESSIVE SHYNESS, REJECTION SENSITIVITY, AND CONFLICTING VALUES THAT YOU EXPERIENCE DUE TO THE EFFECTS OF RSD ON YOUR PSYCHE.

VALIDATE YOUR FEELINGS EVERY DAY, SET BOUNDARIES TO MAINTAIN YOUR SELF-ESTEEM AND PROTECT YOURSELF FROM PSYCHOLOGICAL HARM, IN THE MEDIUM TERM, CREATE A SUPPORT NETWORK OF VERY TRUSTED FRIENDS AND SHOW ON THIS SHEET HOW THIS WILL HELP YOU AND WRITE DOWN THEIR CONTRIBUTIONS AND ENCOURAGEMENT TO DEAL WITH RSD, DON'T FORGET TO PRACTICE DAILY SELF-COMPASSION AFFIRMATIONS, WRITE DOWN YOUR CORE VALUES AND HOW YOU PRIORITIZE YOUR PSYCHOLOGICAL AND EMOTIONAL NEEDS.
DON'T FORGET TO CELEBRATE YOUR PROGRESS ALONG THE WAY AND YOUR DAILY VICTORIES AGAINST RSD!

_____

_____

_____

_____

_____

_____

_____

_____

_____

_____

_____

_____

_____

_____

_____

_____

_____

# RSD-ADHD
# OPPOSITE ACTION PLAN WORKSHEET

*THIS WORKSHEET IS INTENDED TO HELP YOU ACT AGAINST UNHELPFUL EMOTIONAL URGES, ESPECIALLY THOSE THAT MAY LEAD TO ISOLATION, AVOIDANCE, OR IMPULSIVE BEHAVIORS. DIRECTIONS: WHEN YOU FEEL A STRONG EMOTION (ESPECIALLY AN ADHD-RELATED EMOTION SUCH AS REJECTION), IDENTIFY AN OPPOSING ACTION—SOMETHING THAT HELPS BALANCE THE URGE. FOLLOW THE PLAN BELOW.*

| Emotions | Emotion Urge (What do you want to do?) | Opposite Action (What can you do instead?) | How Do You Feel After? |
|---|---|---|---|
|  |  |  |  |
|  |  |  |  |
|  |  |  |  |
|  |  |  |  |
|  |  |  |  |
|  |  |  |  |

# RSD
# INTERACTIONS WORKSHEET

START YOUR DAY WITH A POSITIVE AFFIRMATION AND TACKLE A SMALL, SIMPLE TASK TO GIVE YOURSELF A QUICK SENSE OF ACCOMPLISHMENT. BREAK LARGER TASKS INTO MANAGEABLE STEPS AND SET TIMERS FOR FOCUSED WORK, TAKING SHORT BREAKS IN BETWEEN TO AVOID FEELING OVERWHELMED. REGULARLY CHECK IN WITH YOUR EMOTIONS, ESPECIALLY AFTER TASKS, AND BE KIND TO YOURSELF IF FEELINGS OF REJECTION OR FRUSTRATION ARISE—IT'S OKAY TO FEEL THOSE THINGS. ACKNOWLEDGE ANY CHALLENGES, AND END THE DAY WITH A POSITIVE AFFIRMATION.

Sleep Quality:

## MOOD TRACKER

| | |
|---|---|
| ANGRY | ☐ |
| UPSET | ☐ |
| ANXIOUS | ☐ |
| EMBARRASSED | ☐ |
| UNCOMFORTABLE | ☐ |
| BRAVE | ☐ |
| CALM | ☐ |
| JOYFUL | ☐ |
| PEACEFUL | ☐ |
| CONFUSED | ☐ |
| DISCOURAGED | ☐ |
| DISTRACTED | ☐ |
| EMBARRASSED | ☐ |
| EXCITED | ☐ |
| FRIENDLY | ☐ |
| GUILTY | ☐ |
| HAPPY | ☐ |
| HOPEFUL | ☐ |
| LONELY | ☐ |
| LOVED | ☐ |
| NERVOUS | ☐ |
| OFFENDED | ☐ |
| SCARED | ☐ |
| THOUGHTFUL | ☐ |
| TIRED | ☐ |
| UNCOMFORTABLE | ☐ |
| INSECURE | ☐ |

THINGS TO WORK ON

# OVERCOMING RSD
# PRACTICAL WORKSHEET

Engage in a social situation that you think will enhance your RSD symptoms. Try to interact in a healthy way and remain in control of your feelings outwardly without withdrawing or getting angry. Maintain your self-respect and faith in yourself in situations that require this.

Be bold and engage in situations that reinforce your preconceived sense of failure. Gradually exposing and analyzing these situations enables you to get rid of psychological fragility, build your self-esteem, and gain social intelligence.

| WRITE THE MOST IMPORTANT DETAILS OF THE SITUATION IN THE CORRESPONDING BOX. | EVALUATE YOUR REACTIONS AND INTERACTIONS. (GOOD DEALING AND BAD DEALING) |
|---|---|
| | 👍 |
| | ✋ |

DATE :        /        /

## EXPOSURE THERAPY
## FOR RSD TRAITS

Before engaging in social situations that might trigger RSD, take a moment to plan how you will handle potential emotional triggers. You may want to remind yourself that every comment or interaction is not a reflection of your worth, and that it's okay to step back if you start to feel overwhelmed. Visualizing how you would react to certain situations can help reduce anxiety and give you a sense of control. After the event, use the second part of the chart to assess how well you managed your emotional responses to perceived rejection or criticism, and to assess your level of control over any triggers.

*WHAT SHOULD I DO :*

| | Evaluating my success rate in controlling feelings of rejection or criticism <br> ○ ○ ○ ○ ○ |
|---|---|
| | Evaluating my success rate in showing balance and self-respect <br> ○ ○ ○ ○ ○ |
| | Evaluating my success rate in avoiding false perfection to avoid failure <br> ○ ○ ○ ○ ○ |

## NOTES

# RSD DIALECTICAL WORKSHEET

*Date* .............................................

CHALLENGE AND CORRECT NEGATIVE BEHAVIOR PATTERNS
AND THOUGHTS

ON THIS WORKSHEET, START THINKING ABOUT YOUR TRIGGERS FOR ANXIETY, EXCESSIVE SHYNESS, REJECTION SENSITIVITY, AND CONFLICTING VALUES THAT YOU EXPERIENCE DUE TO THE EFFECTS OF RSD ON YOUR PSYCHE.

VALIDATE YOUR FEELINGS EVERY DAY, SET BOUNDARIES TO MAINTAIN YOUR SELF-ESTEEM AND PROTECT YOURSELF FROM PSYCHOLOGICAL HARM, IN THE MEDIUM TERM, CREATE A SUPPORT NETWORK OF VERY TRUSTED FRIENDS AND SHOW ON THIS SHEET HOW THIS WILL HELP YOU AND WRITE DOWN THEIR CONTRIBUTIONS AND ENCOURAGEMENT TO DEAL WITH RSD, DON'T FORGET TO PRACTICE DAILY SELF-COMPASSION AFFIRMATIONS, WRITE DOWN YOUR CORE VALUES AND HOW YOU PRIORITIZE YOUR PSYCHOLOGICAL AND EMOTIONAL NEEDS.
DON'T FORGET TO CELEBRATE YOUR PROGRESS ALONG THE WAY AND YOUR DAILY VICTORIES AGAINST RSD!

# RSD-ADHD
# OPPOSITE ACTION PLAN WORKSHEET

*THIS WORKSHEET IS INTENDED TO HELP YOU ACT AGAINST UNHELPFUL EMOTIONAL URGES, ESPECIALLY THOSE THAT MAY LEAD TO ISOLATION, AVOIDANCE, OR IMPULSIVE BEHAVIORS. DIRECTIONS: WHEN YOU FEEL A STRONG EMOTION (ESPECIALLY AN ADHD-RELATED EMOTION SUCH AS REJECTION), IDENTIFY AN OPPOSING ACTION—SOMETHING THAT HELPS BALANCE THE URGE. FOLLOW THE PLAN BELOW.*

| Emotions | Emotion Urge (What do you want to do?) | Opposite Action (What can you do instead?) | How Do You Feel After? |
|---|---|---|---|
|  |  |  |  |
|  |  |  |  |
|  |  |  |  |
|  |  |  |  |
|  |  |  |  |
|  |  |  |  |

# RSD
# INTERACTIONS WORKSHEET

START YOUR DAY WITH A POSITIVE AFFIRMATION AND TACKLE A SMALL, SIMPLE TASK TO GIVE YOURSELF A QUICK SENSE OF ACCOMPLISHMENT. BREAK LARGER TASKS INTO MANAGEABLE STEPS AND SET TIMERS FOR FOCUSED WORK, TAKING SHORT BREAKS IN BETWEEN TO AVOID FEELING OVERWHELMED. REGULARLY CHECK IN WITH YOUR EMOTIONS, ESPECIALLY AFTER TASKS, AND BE KIND TO YOURSELF IF FEELINGS OF REJECTION OR FRUSTRATION ARISE—IT'S OKAY TO FEEL THOSE THINGS. ACKNOWLEDGE ANY CHALLENGES, AND END THE DAY WITH A POSITIVE AFFIRMATION.

## MOOD TRACKER ✓

| | |
|---|---|
| ANGRY | ☐ |
| UPSET | ☐ |
| ANXIOUS | ☐ |
| EMBARRASSED | ☐ |
| UNCOMFORTABLE | ☐ |
| BRAVE | ☐ |
| CALM | ☐ |
| JOYFUL | ☐ |
| PEACEFUL | ☐ |
| CONFUSED | ☐ |
| DISCOURAGED | ☐ |
| DISTRACTED | ☐ |
| EMBARRASSED | ☐ |
| EXCITED | ☐ |
| FRIENDLY | ☐ |
| GUILTY | ☐ |
| HAPPY | ☐ |
| HOPEFUL | ☐ |
| LONELY | ☐ |
| LOVED | ☐ |
| NERVOUS | ☐ |
| OFFENDED | ☐ |
| SCARED | ☐ |
| THOUGHTFUL | ☐ |
| TIRED | ☐ |
| UNCOMFORTABLE | ☐ |
| INSECURE | ☐ |

## THINGS TO WORK ON

# OVERCOMING RSD
# PRACTICAL WORKSHEET

Engage in a social situation that you think will enhance your RSD symptoms. Try to interact in a healthy way and remain in control of your feelings outwardly without withdrawing or getting angry. Maintain your self-respect and faith in yourself in situations that require this.

Be bold and engage in situations that reinforce your preconceived sense of failure. Gradually exposing and analyzing these situations enables you to get rid of psychological fragility, build your self-esteem, and gain social intelligence.

| WRITE THE MOST IMPORTANT DETAILS OF THE SITUATION IN THE CORRESPONDING BOX. | EVALUATE YOUR REACTIONS AND INTERACTIONS. (GOOD DEALING AND BAD DEALING) |
|---|---|
| | |

DATE :        /        /

# EXPOSURE THERAPY FOR RSD TRAITS

Before engaging in social situations that might trigger RSD, take a moment to plan how you will handle potential emotional triggers. You may want to remind yourself that every comment or interaction is not a reflection of your worth, and that it's okay to step back if you start to feel overwhelmed. Visualizing how you would react to certain situations can help reduce anxiety and give you a sense of control. After the event, use the second part of the chart to assess how well you managed your emotional responses to perceived rejection or criticism, and to assess your level of control over any triggers.

*WHAT SHOULD I DO :*

| | Evaluating my success rate in controlling feelings of rejection or criticism $\bigcirc \bigcirc \bigcirc \bigcirc \bigcirc$ |
|---|---|
| | Evaluating my success rate in showing balance and self-respect $\bigcirc \bigcirc \bigcirc \bigcirc \bigcirc$ |
| | Evaluating my success rate in avoiding false perfection to avoid failure $\bigcirc \bigcirc \bigcirc \bigcirc \bigcirc$ |

## NOTES

# RSD DIALECTICAL WORKSHEET

CHALLENGE AND CORRECT NEGATIVE BEHAVIOR PATTERNS
AND THOUGHTS

ON THIS WORKSHEET, START THINKING ABOUT YOUR TRIGGERS FOR ANXIETY, EXCESSIVE SHYNESS, REJECTION SENSITIVITY, AND CONFLICTING VALUES THAT YOU EXPERIENCE DUE TO THE EFFECTS OF RSD ON YOUR PSYCHE.

VALIDATE YOUR FEELINGS EVERY DAY, SET BOUNDARIES TO MAINTAIN YOUR SELF-ESTEEM AND PROTECT YOURSELF FROM PSYCHOLOGICAL HARM, IN THE MEDIUM TERM, CREATE A SUPPORT NETWORK OF VERY TRUSTED FRIENDS AND SHOW ON THIS SHEET HOW THIS WILL HELP YOU AND WRITE DOWN THEIR CONTRIBUTIONS AND ENCOURAGEMENT TO DEAL WITH RSD, DON'T FORGET TO PRACTICE DAILY SELF-COMPASSION AFFIRMATIONS, WRITE DOWN YOUR CORE VALUES AND HOW YOU PRIORITIZE YOUR PSYCHOLOGICAL AND EMOTIONAL NEEDS.
DON'T FORGET TO CELEBRATE YOUR PROGRESS ALONG THE WAY AND YOUR DAILY VICTORIES AGAINST RSD!

_____
_____
_____
_____
_____
_____
_____
_____
_____
_____
_____
_____
_____
_____
_____
_____
_____
_____

THIS WORKSHEET IS INTENDED TO HELP YOU ACT AGAINST UNHELPFUL EMOTIONAL URGES, ESPECIALLY THOSE THAT MAY LEAD TO ISOLATION, AVOIDANCE, OR IMPULSIVE BEHAVIORS. DIRECTIONS: WHEN YOU FEEL A STRONG EMOTION (ESPECIALLY AN ADHD-RELATED EMOTION SUCH AS REJECTION), IDENTIFY AN OPPOSING ACTION—SOMETHING THAT HELPS BALANCE THE URGE. FOLLOW THE PLAN BELOW.

| Emotions | Emotion Urge (What do you want to do?) | Opposite Action (What can you do instead?) | How Do You Feel After? |
|---|---|---|---|
|  |  |  |  |
|  |  |  |  |
|  |  |  |  |
|  |  |  |  |
|  |  |  |  |
|  |  |  |  |

Date : / /

Sleep Quality:

START YOUR DAY WITH A POSITIVE AFFIRMATION AND TACKLE A SMALL, SIMPLE TASK TO GIVE YOURSELF A QUICK SENSE OF ACCOMPLISHMENT. BREAK LARGER TASKS INTO MANAGEABLE STEPS AND SET TIMERS FOR FOCUSED WORK, TAKING SHORT BREAKS IN BETWEEN TO AVOID FEELING OVERWHELMED. REGULARLY CHECK IN WITH YOUR EMOTIONS, ESPECIALLY AFTER TASKS, AND BE KIND TO YOURSELF IF FEELINGS OF REJECTION OR FRUSTRATION ARISE—IT'S OKAY TO FEEL THOSE THINGS. ACKNOWLEDGE ANY CHALLENGES, AND END THE DAY WITH A POSITIVE AFFIRMATION.

✓ ___ : ___

✓ ___ : ___

## THINGS TO WORK ON

## MOOD TRACKER ✓

- [ ] ANGRY
- [ ] UPSET
- [ ] ANXIOUS
- [ ] EMBARRASSED
- [ ] UNCOMFORTABLE
- [ ] BRAVE
- [ ] CALM
- [ ] JOYFUL
- [ ] PEACEFUL
- [ ] CONFUSED
- [ ] DISCOURAGED
- [ ] DISTRACTED
- [ ] EMBARRASSED
- [ ] EXCITED
- [ ] FRIENDLY
- [ ] GUILTY
- [ ] HAPPY
- [ ] HOPEFUL
- [ ] LONELY
- [ ] LOVED
- [ ] NERVOUS
- [ ] OFFENDED
- [ ] SCARED
- [ ] THOUGHTFUL
- [ ] TIRED
- [ ] UNCOMFORTABLE
- [ ] INSECURE

# OVERCOMING RSD PRACTICAL WORKSHEET

Engage in a social situation that you think will enhance your RSD symptoms. Try to interact in a healthy way and remain in control of your feelings outwardly without withdrawing or getting angry. Maintain your self-respect and faith in yourself in situations that require this.

Be bold and engage in situations that reinforce your preconceived sense of failure. Gradually exposing and analyzing these situations enables you to get rid of psychological fragility, build your self-esteem, and gain social intelligence.

| WRITE THE MOST IMPORTANT DETAILS OF THE SITUATION IN THE CORRESPONDING BOX. | EVALUATE YOUR REACTIONS AND INTERACTIONS. (GOOD DEALING AND BAD DEALING) |
|---|---|
| | 👍 |
| | ✋ |

DATE :          /          /

Before engaging in social situations that might trigger RSD, take a moment to plan how you will handle potential emotional triggers. You may want to remind yourself that every comment or interaction is not a reflection of your worth, and that it's okay to step back if you start to feel overwhelmed. Visualizing how you would react to certain situations can help reduce anxiety and give you a sense of control. After the event, use the second part of the chart to assess how well you managed your emotional responses to perceived rejection or criticism, and to assess your level of control over any triggers.

*WHAT SHOULD I DO :*

| | |
|---|---|
| | Evaluating my success rate in controlling feelings of rejection or criticism <br> ○ ○ ○ ○ ○ |
| | Evaluating my success rate in showing balance and self-respect <br> ○ ○ ○ ○ ○ |
| | Evaluating my success rate in avoiding false perfection to avoid failure <br> ○ ○ ○ ○ ○ |

NOTES

# RSD DIALECTICAL WORKSHEET

*Date*

ON THIS WORKSHEET, START THINKING ABOUT YOUR TRIGGERS FOR ANXIETY, EXCESSIVE SHYNESS, REJECTION SENSITIVITY, AND CONFLICTING VALUES THAT YOU EXPERIENCE DUE TO THE EFFECTS OF RSD ON YOUR PSYCHE.

VALIDATE YOUR FEELINGS EVERY DAY, SET BOUNDARIES TO MAINTAIN YOUR SELF-ESTEEM AND PROTECT YOURSELF FROM PSYCHOLOGICAL HARM, IN THE MEDIUM TERM, CREATE A SUPPORT NETWORK OF VERY TRUSTED FRIENDS AND SHOW ON THIS SHEET HOW THIS WILL HELP YOU AND WRITE DOWN THEIR CONTRIBUTIONS AND ENCOURAGEMENT TO DEAL WITH RSD, DON'T FORGET TO PRACTICE DAILY SELF-COMPASSION AFFIRMATIONS, WRITE DOWN YOUR CORE VALUES AND HOW YOU PRIORITIZE YOUR PSYCHOLOGICAL AND EMOTIONAL NEEDS.
DON'T FORGET TO CELEBRATE YOUR PROGRESS ALONG THE WAY AND YOUR DAILY VICTORIES AGAINST RSD!

*THIS WORKSHEET IS INTENDED TO HELP YOU ACT AGAINST UNHELPFUL EMOTIONAL URGES, ESPECIALLY THOSE THAT MAY LEAD TO ISOLATION, AVOIDANCE, OR IMPULSIVE BEHAVIORS. DIRECTIONS: WHEN YOU FEEL A STRONG EMOTION (ESPECIALLY AN ADHD-RELATED EMOTION SUCH AS REJECTION), IDENTIFY AN OPPOSING ACTION—SOMETHING THAT HELPS BALANCE THE URGE. FOLLOW THE PLAN BELOW.*

| Emotions | Emotion Urge (What do you want to do?) | Opposite Action (What can you do instead?) | How Do You Feel After? |
|---|---|---|---|
|  |  |  |  |
|  |  |  |  |
|  |  |  |  |
|  |  |  |  |
|  |  |  |  |
|  |  |  |  |

# RSD
# INTERACTIONS WORKSHEET

START YOUR DAY WITH A POSITIVE AFFIRMATION AND TACKLE A SMALL, SIMPLE TASK TO GIVE YOURSELF A QUICK SENSE OF ACCOMPLISHMENT. BREAK LARGER TASKS INTO MANAGEABLE STEPS AND SET TIMERS FOR FOCUSED WORK, TAKING SHORT BREAKS IN BETWEEN TO AVOID FEELING OVERWHELMED. REGULARLY CHECK IN WITH YOUR EMOTIONS, ESPECIALLY AFTER TASKS, AND BE KIND TO YOURSELF IF FEELINGS OF REJECTION OR FRUSTRATION ARISE—IT'S OKAY TO FEEL THOSE THINGS. ACKNOWLEDGE ANY CHALLENGES, AND END THE DAY WITH A POSITIVE AFFIRMATION.

Sleep Quality:

## MOOD TRACKER ✓

| | |
|---|---|
| ANGRY | ☐ |
| UPSET | ☐ |
| ANXIOUS | ☐ |
| EMBARRASSED | ☐ |
| UNCOMFORTABLE | ☐ |
| BRAVE | ☐ |
| CALM | ☐ |
| JOYFUL | ☐ |
| PEACEFUL | ☐ |
| CONFUSED | ☐ |
| DISCOURAGED | ☐ |
| DISTRACTED | ☐ |
| EMBARRASSED | ☐ |
| EXCITED | ☐ |
| FRIENDLY | ☐ |
| GUILTY | ☐ |
| HAPPY | ☐ |
| HOPEFUL | ☐ |
| LONELY | ☐ |
| LOVED | ☐ |
| NERVOUS | ☐ |
| OFFENDED | ☐ |
| SCARED | ☐ |
| THOUGHTFUL | ☐ |
| TIRED | ☐ |
| UNCOMFORTABLE | ☐ |
| INSECURE | ☐ |

⊘ ____ : ____

⊘ ____ : ____

## THINGS TO WORK ON

# OVERCOMING RSD
# PRACTICAL WORKSHEET

Engage in a social situation that you think will enhance your RSD symptoms. Try to interact in a healthy way and remain in control of your feelings outwardly without withdrawing or getting angry. Maintain your self-respect and faith in yourself in situations that require this.
Be bold and engage in situations that reinforce your preconceived sense of failure. Gradually exposing and analyzing these situations enables you to get rid of psychological fragility, build your self-esteem, and gain social intelligence.

| WRITE THE MOST IMPORTANT DETAILS OF THE SITUATION IN THE CORRESPONDING BOX. | EVALUATE YOUR REACTIONS AND INTERACTIONS. (GOOD DEALING AND BAD DEALING) |
|---|---|
| | 👍 |
| | ✋ |

# EXPOSURE THERAPY
# FOR RSD TRAITS

Before engaging in social situations that might trigger RSD, take a moment to plan how you will handle potential emotional triggers. You may want to remind yourself that every comment or interaction is not a reflection of your worth, and that it's okay to step back if you start to feel overwhelmed. Visualizing how you would react to certain situations can help reduce anxiety and give you a sense of control. After the event, use the second part of the chart to assess how well you managed your emotional responses to perceived rejection or criticism, and to assess your level of control over any triggers.

*WHAT SHOULD I DO :*

| | |
|---|---|
| | Evaluating my success rate in controlling feelings of rejection or criticism<br><br>○ ○ ○ ○ ○ |
| | Evaluating my success rate in showing balance and self-respect<br><br>○ ○ ○ ○ ○ |
| | Evaluating my success rate in avoiding false perfection to avoid failure<br><br>○ ○ ○ ○ ○ |

# NOTES

# RSD DIALECTICAL WORKSHEET

CHALLENGE AND CORRECT NEGATIVE BEHAVIOR PATTERNS
AND THOUGHTS

ON THIS WORKSHEET, START THINKING ABOUT YOUR TRIGGERS FOR ANXIETY, EXCESSIVE SHYNESS,
REJECTION SENSITIVITY, AND CONFLICTING VALUES THAT YOU EXPERIENCE DUE TO THE EFFECTS OF RSD ON
YOUR PSYCHE.

VALIDATE YOUR FEELINGS EVERY DAY, SET BOUNDARIES TO MAINTAIN YOUR SELF-ESTEEM AND PROTECT
YOURSELF FROM PSYCHOLOGICAL HARM, IN THE MEDIUM TERM, CREATE A SUPPORT NETWORK OF VERY
TRUSTED FRIENDS AND SHOW ON THIS SHEET HOW THIS WILL HELP YOU AND WRITE DOWN THEIR
CONTRIBUTIONS AND ENCOURAGEMENT TO DEAL WITH RSD, DON'T FORGET TO PRACTICE DAILY
SELF-COMPASSION AFFIRMATIONS, WRITE DOWN YOUR CORE VALUES AND HOW YOU PRIORITIZE YOUR
PSYCHOLOGICAL AND EMOTIONAL NEEDS.
DON'T FORGET TO CELEBRATE YOUR PROGRESS ALONG THE WAY AND YOUR DAILY VICTORIES AGAINST RSD!

_____

_____

_____

_____

_____

_____

_____

_____

_____

_____

_____

_____

_____

_____

_____

_____

# RSD-ADHD
# OPPOSITE ACTION PLAN WORKSHEET

THIS WORKSHEET IS INTENDED TO HELP YOU ACT AGAINST UNHELPFUL EMOTIONAL URGES, ESPECIALLY THOSE THAT MAY LEAD TO ISOLATION, AVOIDANCE, OR IMPULSIVE BEHAVIORS. DIRECTIONS: WHEN YOU FEEL A STRONG EMOTION (ESPECIALLY AN ADHD-RELATED EMOTION SUCH AS REJECTION), IDENTIFY AN OPPOSING ACTION—SOMETHING THAT HELPS BALANCE THE URGE. FOLLOW THE PLAN BELOW.

| Emotions | Emotion Urge (What do you want to do?) | Opposite Action (What can you do instead?) | How Do You Feel After? |
|---|---|---|---|
|  |  |  |  |
|  |  |  |  |
|  |  |  |  |
|  |  |  |  |
|  |  |  |  |
|  |  |  |  |

# RSD
# INTERACTIONS WORKSHEET

START YOUR DAY WITH A POSITIVE AFFIRMATION AND TACKLE A SMALL, SIMPLE TASK TO GIVE YOURSELF A QUICK SENSE OF ACCOMPLISHMENT. BREAK LARGER TASKS INTO MANAGEABLE STEPS AND SET TIMERS FOR FOCUSED WORK, TAKING SHORT BREAKS IN BETWEEN TO AVOID FEELING OVERWHELMED. REGULARLY CHECK IN WITH YOUR EMOTIONS, ESPECIALLY AFTER TASKS, AND BE KIND TO YOURSELF IF FEELINGS OF REJECTION OR FRUSTRATION ARISE—IT'S OKAY TO FEEL THOSE THINGS. ACKNOWLEDGE ANY CHALLENGES, AND END THE DAY WITH A POSITIVE AFFIRMATION.

✓ ___ : ___

✓ ___ : ___

## THINGS TO WORK ON

Sleep Quality:

## MOOD TRACKER ✓

| | |
|---|---|
| ANGRY | ☐ |
| UPSET | ☐ |
| ANXIOUS | ☐ |
| EMBARRASSED | ☐ |
| UNCOMFORTABLE | ☐ |
| BRAVE | ☐ |
| CALM | ☐ |
| JOYFUL | ☐ |
| PEACEFUL | ☐ |
| CONFUSED | ☐ |
| DISCOURAGED | ☐ |
| DISTRACTED | ☐ |
| EMBARRASSED | ☐ |
| EXCITED | ☐ |
| FRIENDLY | ☐ |
| GUILTY | ☐ |
| HAPPY | ☐ |
| HOPEFUL | ☐ |
| LONELY | ☐ |
| LOVED | ☐ |
| NERVOUS | ☐ |
| OFFENDED | ☐ |
| SCARED | ☐ |
| THOUGHTFUL | ☐ |
| TIRED | ☐ |
| UNCOMFORTABLE | ☐ |
| INSECURE | ☐ |

# OVERCOMING RSD PRACTICAL WORKSHEET

Engage in a social situation that you think will enhance your RSD symptoms. Try to interact in a healthy way and remain in control of your feelings outwardly without withdrawing or getting angry. Maintain your self-respect and faith in yourself in situations that require this.

Be bold and engage in situations that reinforce your preconceived sense of failure. Gradually exposing and analyzing these situations enables you to get rid of psychological fragility, build your self-esteem, and gain social intelligence.

| WRITE THE MOST IMPORTANT DETAILS OF THE SITUATION IN THE CORRESPONDING BOX. | EVALUATE YOUR REACTIONS AND INTERACTIONS. (GOOD DEALING AND BAD DEALING) |
|---|---|
| | |

DATE :          /          /

## EXPOSURE THERAPY FOR RSD TRAITS

Before engaging in social situations that might trigger RSD, take a moment to plan how you will handle potential emotional triggers. You may want to remind yourself that every comment or interaction is not a reflection of your worth, and that it's okay to step back if you start to feel overwhelmed. Visualizing how you would react to certain situations can help reduce anxiety and give you a sense of control. After the event, use the second part of the chart to assess how well you managed your emotional responses to perceived rejection or criticism, and to assess your level of control over any triggers.

*WHAT SHOULD I DO :*

|  |  |
|---|---|
|  | Evaluating my success rate in controlling feelings of rejection or criticism<br><br>○ ○ ○ ○ ○ |
|  | Evaluating my success rate in showing balance and self-respect<br><br>○ ○ ○ ○ ○ |
|  | Evaluating my success rate in avoiding false perfection to avoid failure<br><br>○ ○ ○ ○ ○ |

## NOTES

_____

_____

_____

# RSD DIALECTICAL WORKSHEET

Date

CHALLENGE AND CORRECT NEGATIVE BEHAVIOR PATTERNS
AND THOUGHTS

ON THIS WORKSHEET, START THINKING ABOUT YOUR TRIGGERS FOR ANXIETY, EXCESSIVE SHYNESS, REJECTION SENSITIVITY, AND CONFLICTING VALUES THAT YOU EXPERIENCE DUE TO THE EFFECTS OF RSD ON YOUR PSYCHE.

VALIDATE YOUR FEELINGS EVERY DAY, SET BOUNDARIES TO MAINTAIN YOUR SELF-ESTEEM AND PROTECT YOURSELF FROM PSYCHOLOGICAL HARM, IN THE MEDIUM TERM, CREATE A SUPPORT NETWORK OF VERY TRUSTED FRIENDS AND SHOW ON THIS SHEET HOW THIS WILL HELP YOU AND WRITE DOWN THEIR CONTRIBUTIONS AND ENCOURAGEMENT TO DEAL WITH RSD, DON'T FORGET TO PRACTICE DAILY SELF-COMPASSION AFFIRMATIONS, WRITE DOWN YOUR CORE VALUES AND HOW YOU PRIORITIZE YOUR PSYCHOLOGICAL AND EMOTIONAL NEEDS.
DON'T FORGET TO CELEBRATE YOUR PROGRESS ALONG THE WAY AND YOUR DAILY VICTORIES AGAINST RSD!

# RSD-ADHD
# OPPOSITE ACTION PLAN WORKSHEET

*THIS WORKSHEET IS INTENDED TO HELP YOU ACT AGAINST UNHELPFUL EMOTIONAL URGES, ESPECIALLY THOSE THAT MAY LEAD TO ISOLATION, AVOIDANCE, OR IMPULSIVE BEHAVIORS. DIRECTIONS: WHEN YOU FEEL A STRONG EMOTION (ESPECIALLY AN ADHD-RELATED EMOTION SUCH AS REJECTION), IDENTIFY AN OPPOSING ACTION—SOMETHING THAT HELPS BALANCE THE URGE. FOLLOW THE PLAN BELOW.*

| Emotions | Emotion Urge (What do you want to do?) | Opposite Action (What can you do instead?) | How Do You Feel After? |
|---|---|---|---|
| | | | |
| | | | |
| | | | |
| | | | |
| | | | |
| | | | |

# RSD
# INTERACTIONS WORKSHEET

START YOUR DAY WITH A POSITIVE AFFIRMATION AND TACKLE A SMALL, SIMPLE TASK TO GIVE YOURSELF A QUICK SENSE OF ACCOMPLISHMENT. BREAK LARGER TASKS INTO MANAGEABLE STEPS AND SET TIMERS FOR FOCUSED WORK, TAKING SHORT BREAKS IN BETWEEN TO AVOID FEELING OVERWHELMED. REGULARLY CHECK IN WITH YOUR EMOTIONS, ESPECIALLY AFTER TASKS, AND BE KIND TO YOURSELF IF FEELINGS OF REJECTION OR FRUSTRATION ARISE—IT'S OKAY TO FEEL THOSE THINGS. ACKNOWLEDGE ANY CHALLENGES, AND END THE DAY WITH A POSITIVE AFFIRMATION.

Sleep Quality:

## MOOD TRACKER ✔

| | |
|---|---|
| ANGRY | ☐ |
| UPSET | ☐ |
| ANXIOUS | ☐ |
| EMBARRASSED | ☐ |
| UNCOMFORTABLE | ☐ |
| BRAVE | ☐ |
| CALM | ☐ |
| JOYFUL | ☐ |
| PEACEFUL | ☐ |
| CONFUSED | ☐ |
| DISCOURAGED | ☐ |
| DISTRACTED | ☐ |
| EMBARRASSED | ☐ |
| EXCITED | ☐ |
| FRIENDLY | ☐ |
| GUILTY | ☐ |
| HAPPY | ☐ |
| HOPEFUL | ☐ |
| LONELY | ☐ |
| LOVED | ☐ |
| NERVOUS | ☐ |
| OFFENDED | ☐ |
| SCARED | ☐ |
| THOUGHTFUL | ☐ |
| TIRED | ☐ |
| UNCOMFORTABLE | ☐ |
| INSECURE | ☐ |

THINGS TO WORK ON

# OVERCOMING RSD PRACTICAL WORKSHEET

Engage in a social situation that you think will enhance your RSD symptoms. Try to interact in a healthy way and remain in control of your feelings outwardly without withdrawing or getting angry. Maintain your self-respect and faith in yourself in situations that require this.
Be bold and engage in situations that reinforce your preconceived sense of failure. Gradually exposing and analyzing these situations enables you to get rid of psychological fragility, build your self-esteem, and gain social intelligence.

| WRITE THE MOST IMPORTANT DETAILS OF THE SITUATION IN THE CORRESPONDING BOX. | EVALUATE YOUR REACTIONS AND INTERACTIONS. (GOOD DEALING AND BAD DEALING) |
|---|---|
| | 👍 |
| | ✋ |

DATE :         /         /

# EXPOSURE THERAPY
# FOR RSD TRAITS

Before engaging in social situations that might trigger RSD, take a moment to plan how you will handle potential emotional triggers. You may want to remind yourself that every comment or interaction is not a reflection of your worth, and that it's okay to step back if you start to feel overwhelmed. Visualizing how you would react to certain situations can help reduce anxiety and give you a sense of control. After the event, use the second part of the chart to assess how well you managed your emotional responses to perceived rejection or criticism, and to assess your level of control over any triggers.

*WHAT SHOULD I DO :*

| | |
|---|---|
| | Evaluating my success rate in controlling feelings of rejection or criticism<br><br>○ ○ ○ ○ ○ |
| | Evaluating my success rate in showing balance and self-respect<br><br>○ ○ ○ ○ ○ |
| | Evaluating my success rate in avoiding false perfection to avoid failure<br><br>○ ○ ○ ○ ○ |

# NOTES

# RSD DIALECTICAL WORKSHEET

CHALLENGE AND CORRECT NEGATIVE BEHAVIOR PATTERNS
AND THOUGHTS

ON THIS WORKSHEET, START THINKING ABOUT YOUR TRIGGERS FOR ANXIETY, EXCESSIVE SHYNESS,
REJECTION SENSITIVITY, AND CONFLICTING VALUES THAT YOU EXPERIENCE DUE TO THE EFFECTS OF RSD ON
YOUR PSYCHE.

VALIDATE YOUR FEELINGS EVERY DAY, SET BOUNDARIES TO MAINTAIN YOUR SELF-ESTEEM AND PROTECT
YOURSELF FROM PSYCHOLOGICAL HARM, IN THE MEDIUM TERM, CREATE A SUPPORT NETWORK OF VERY
TRUSTED FRIENDS AND SHOW ON THIS SHEET HOW THIS WILL HELP YOU AND WRITE DOWN THEIR
CONTRIBUTIONS AND ENCOURAGEMENT TO DEAL WITH RSD, DON'T FORGET TO PRACTICE DAILY
SELF-COMPASSION AFFIRMATIONS, WRITE DOWN YOUR CORE VALUES AND HOW YOU PRIORITIZE YOUR
PSYCHOLOGICAL AND EMOTIONAL NEEDS.
DON'T FORGET TO CELEBRATE YOUR PROGRESS ALONG THE WAY AND YOUR DAILY VICTORIES AGAINST RSD!

# RSD-ADHD
# OPPOSITE ACTION PLAN WORKSHEET

*THIS WORKSHEET IS INTENDED TO HELP YOU ACT AGAINST UNHELPFUL EMOTIONAL URGES, ESPECIALLY THOSE THAT MAY LEAD TO ISOLATION, AVOIDANCE, OR IMPULSIVE BEHAVIORS. DIRECTIONS: WHEN YOU FEEL A STRONG EMOTION (ESPECIALLY AN ADHD-RELATED EMOTION SUCH AS REJECTION), IDENTIFY AN OPPOSING ACTION—SOMETHING THAT HELPS BALANCE THE URGE. FOLLOW THE PLAN BELOW.*

| Emotions | Emotion Urge (What do you want to do?) | Opposite Action (What can you do instead?) | How Do You Feel After? |
|---|---|---|---|
|  |  |  |  |
|  |  |  |  |
|  |  |  |  |
|  |  |  |  |
|  |  |  |  |
|  |  |  |  |

# RSD
# INTERACTIONS WORKSHEET

START YOUR DAY WITH A POSITIVE AFFIRMATION AND TACKLE A SMALL, SIMPLE TASK TO GIVE YOURSELF A QUICK SENSE OF ACCOMPLISHMENT. BREAK LARGER TASKS INTO MANAGEABLE STEPS AND SET TIMERS FOR FOCUSED WORK, TAKING SHORT BREAKS IN BETWEEN TO AVOID FEELING OVERWHELMED. REGULARLY CHECK IN WITH YOUR EMOTIONS, ESPECIALLY AFTER TASKS, AND BE KIND TO YOURSELF IF FEELINGS OF REJECTION OR FRUSTRATION ARISE—IT'S OKAY TO FEEL THOSE THINGS. ACKNOWLEDGE ANY CHALLENGES, AND END THE DAY WITH A POSITIVE AFFIRMATION.

✓ ___ : ___

✓ ___ : ___

## THINGS TO WORK ON

## MOOD TRACKER ✓

| | |
|---|---|
| ANGRY | ☐ |
| UPSET | ☐ |
| ANXIOUS | ☐ |
| EMBARRASSED | ☐ |
| UNCOMFORTABLE | ☐ |
| BRAVE | ☐ |
| CALM | ☐ |
| JOYFUL | ☐ |
| PEACEFUL | ☐ |
| CONFUSED | ☐ |
| DISCOURAGED | ☐ |
| DISTRACTED | ☐ |
| EMBARRASSED | ☐ |
| EXCITED | ☐ |
| FRIENDLY | ☐ |
| GUILTY | ☐ |
| HAPPY | ☐ |
| HOPEFUL | ☐ |
| LONELY | ☐ |
| LOVED | ☐ |
| NERVOUS | ☐ |
| OFFENDED | ☐ |
| SCARED | ☐ |
| THOUGHTFUL | ☐ |
| TIRED | ☐ |
| UNCOMFORTABLE | ☐ |
| INSECURE | ☐ |

# OVERCOMING RSD
# PRACTICAL WORKSHEET

Engage in a social situation that you think will enhance your RSD symptoms. Try to interact in a healthy way and remain in control of your feelings outwardly without withdrawing or getting angry. Maintain your self-respect and faith in yourself in situations that require this.
Be bold and engage in situations that reinforce your preconceived sense of failure. Gradually exposing and analyzing these situations enables you to get rid of psychological fragility, build your self-esteem, and gain social intelligence.

| WRITE THE MOST IMPORTANT DETAILS OF THE SITUATION IN THE CORRESPONDING BOX. | EVALUATE YOUR REACTIONS AND INTERACTIONS. (GOOD DEALING AND BAD DEALING) |
|---|---|
| | |

DATE :        /        /

# EXPOSURE THERAPY
# FOR RSD TRAITS

Before engaging in social situations that might trigger RSD, take a moment to plan how you will handle potential emotional triggers. You may want to remind yourself that every comment or interaction is not a reflection of your worth, and that it's okay to step back if you start to feel overwhelmed. Visualizing how you would react to certain situations can help reduce anxiety and give you a sense of control. After the event, use the second part of the chart to assess how well you managed your emotional responses to perceived rejection or criticism, and to assess your level of control over any triggers.

*WHAT SHOULD I DO :*

| | Evaluating my success rate in controlling feelings of rejection or criticism<br>〇 〇 〇 〇 〇 |
|---|---|
| | Evaluating my success rate in showing balance and self-respect<br>〇 〇 〇 〇 〇 |
| | Evaluating my success rate in avoiding false perfection to avoid failure<br>〇 〇 〇 〇 〇 |

NOTES

# RSD DIALECTICAL WORKSHEET

CHALLENGE AND CORRECT NEGATIVE BEHAVIOR PATTERNS AND THOUGHTS

ON THIS WORKSHEET, START THINKING ABOUT YOUR TRIGGERS FOR ANXIETY, EXCESSIVE SHYNESS, REJECTION SENSITIVITY, AND CONFLICTING VALUES THAT YOU EXPERIENCE DUE TO THE EFFECTS OF RSD ON YOUR PSYCHE.

VALIDATE YOUR FEELINGS EVERY DAY, SET BOUNDARIES TO MAINTAIN YOUR SELF-ESTEEM AND PROTECT YOURSELF FROM PSYCHOLOGICAL HARM, IN THE MEDIUM TERM, CREATE A SUPPORT NETWORK OF VERY TRUSTED FRIENDS AND SHOW ON THIS SHEET HOW THIS WILL HELP YOU AND WRITE DOWN THEIR CONTRIBUTIONS AND ENCOURAGEMENT TO DEAL WITH RSD, DON'T FORGET TO PRACTICE DAILY SELF-COMPASSION AFFIRMATIONS, WRITE DOWN YOUR CORE VALUES AND HOW YOU PRIORITIZE YOUR PSYCHOLOGICAL AND EMOTIONAL NEEDS.
DON'T FORGET TO CELEBRATE YOUR PROGRESS ALONG THE WAY AND YOUR DAILY VICTORIES AGAINST RSD!

# RSD-ADHD
# OPPOSITE ACTION PLAN WORKSHEET

THIS WORKSHEET IS INTENDED TO HELP YOU ACT AGAINST UNHELPFUL EMOTIONAL URGES, ESPECIALLY THOSE THAT MAY LEAD TO ISOLATION, AVOIDANCE, OR IMPULSIVE BEHAVIORS. DIRECTIONS: WHEN YOU FEEL A STRONG EMOTION (ESPECIALLY AN ADHD-RELATED EMOTION SUCH AS REJECTION), IDENTIFY AN OPPOSING ACTION—SOMETHING THAT HELPS BALANCE THE URGE. FOLLOW THE PLAN BELOW.

| Emotions | Emotion Urge (What do you want to do?) | Opposite Action (What can you do instead?) | How Do You Feel After? |
|---|---|---|---|
|  |  |  |  |
|  |  |  |  |
|  |  |  |  |
|  |  |  |  |
|  |  |  |  |
|  |  |  |  |

START YOUR DAY WITH A POSITIVE AFFIRMATION AND TACKLE A SMALL, SIMPLE TASK TO GIVE YOURSELF A QUICK SENSE OF ACCOMPLISHMENT. BREAK LARGER TASKS INTO MANAGEABLE STEPS AND SET TIMERS FOR FOCUSED WORK, TAKING SHORT BREAKS IN BETWEEN TO AVOID FEELING OVERWHELMED. REGULARLY CHECK IN WITH YOUR EMOTIONS, ESPECIALLY AFTER TASKS, AND BE KIND TO YOURSELF IF FEELINGS OF REJECTION OR FRUSTRATION ARISE—IT'S OKAY TO FEEL THOSE THINGS. ACKNOWLEDGE ANY CHALLENGES, AND END THE DAY WITH A POSITIVE AFFIRMATION.

Date : / /

Sleep Quality:

## MOOD TRACKER ✓

- ANGRY ☐
- UPSET ☐
- ANXIOUS ☐
- EMBARRASSED ☐
- UNCOMFORTABLE ☐
- BRAVE ☐
- CALM ☐
- JOYFUL ☐
- PEACEFUL ☐
- CONFUSED ☐
- DISCOURAGED ☐
- DISTRACTED ☐
- EMBARRASSED ☐
- EXCITED ☐
- FRIENDLY ☐
- GUILTY ☐
- HAPPY ☐
- HOPEFUL ☐
- LONELY ☐
- LOVED ☐
- NERVOUS ☐
- OFFENDED ☐
- SCARED ☐
- THOUGHTFUL ☐
- TIRED ☐
- UNCOMFORTABLE ☐
- INSECURE ☐

____ : ____

____ : ____

## THINGS TO WORK ON

# OVERCOMING RSD PRACTICAL WORKSHEET

Engage in a social situation that you think will enhance your RSD symptoms. Try to interact in a healthy way and remain in control of your feelings outwardly without withdrawing or getting angry. Maintain your self-respect and faith in yourself in situations that require this.

Be bold and engage in situations that reinforce your preconceived sense of failure. Gradually exposing and analyzing these situations enables you to get rid of psychological fragility, build your self-esteem, and gain social intelligence.

| WRITE THE MOST IMPORTANT DETAILS OF THE SITUATION IN THE CORRESPONDING BOX. | EVALUATE YOUR REACTIONS AND INTERACTIONS. (GOOD DEALING AND BAD DEALING) |
|---|---|
| | 👍 |
| | 🤚 |

DATE :        /        /

# EXPOSURE THERAPY
# FOR RSD TRAITS

Before engaging in social situations that might trigger RSD, take a moment to plan how you will handle potential emotional triggers. You may want to remind yourself that every comment or interaction is not a reflection of your worth, and that it's okay to step back if you start to feel overwhelmed. Visualizing how you would react to certain situations can help reduce anxiety and give you a sense of control. After the event, use the second part of the chart to assess how well you managed your emotional responses to perceived rejection or criticism, and to assess your level of control over any triggers.

**WHAT SHOULD I DO :**

| | |
|---|---|
| | Evaluating my success rate in controlling feelings of rejection or criticism ○ ○ ○ ○ ○ |
| | Evaluating my success rate in showing balance and self-respect ○ ○ ○ ○ ○ |
| | Evaluating my success rate in avoiding false perfection to avoid failure ○ ○ ○ ○ ○ |

# NOTES

# RSD DIALECTICAL WORKSHEET

*Date* ........................................................

ON THIS WORKSHEET, START THINKING ABOUT YOUR TRIGGERS FOR ANXIETY, EXCESSIVE SHYNESS, REJECTION SENSITIVITY, AND CONFLICTING VALUES THAT YOU EXPERIENCE DUE TO THE EFFECTS OF RSD ON YOUR PSYCHE.

VALIDATE YOUR FEELINGS EVERY DAY, SET BOUNDARIES TO MAINTAIN YOUR SELF-ESTEEM AND PROTECT YOURSELF FROM PSYCHOLOGICAL HARM, IN THE MEDIUM TERM, CREATE A SUPPORT NETWORK OF VERY TRUSTED FRIENDS AND SHOW ON THIS SHEET HOW THIS WILL HELP YOU AND WRITE DOWN THEIR CONTRIBUTIONS AND ENCOURAGEMENT TO DEAL WITH RSD, DON'T FORGET TO PRACTICE DAILY SELF-COMPASSION AFFIRMATIONS, WRITE DOWN YOUR CORE VALUES AND HOW YOU PRIORITIZE YOUR PSYCHOLOGICAL AND EMOTIONAL NEEDS.
DON'T FORGET TO CELEBRATE YOUR PROGRESS ALONG THE WAY AND YOUR DAILY VICTORIES AGAINST RSD!

_____

_____

_____

_____

_____

_____

_____

_____

_____

_____

_____

_____

_____

_____

_____

_____

_____

_____

Made in the USA
Las Vegas, NV
23 January 2025